Observing
Teaching and Learning

Principles and Practice

Edited by

Christina Tilstone

David Fulton Publishers

London

to Gavin, Vanessa and Justin Tilstone
who taught me so much

David Fulton Publishers Ltd
Ormond House, 26–27 Boswell Street, London WC1N 3JD

First published in Great Britain by David Fulton Publishers 1998

Note: The right of Christina Tilstone to be identified as the editor of this work has been asserted by her in accordance with the Copyright, Designs and Patents Act 1988.

British Library Cataloguing in Publication Data
A catalogue record for this book is available from the British Library

ISBN 1–85346–334–5

Typeset by FSH Print and Production Ltd, London
Printed in Great Britain by BPC Books and Journals Ltd, Exeter

Contents

Preface

In most practical books on teaching and learning, curriculum planning, and assessment, you will find the word 'observation' and the assumption will be made that you know what observation is and how best to approach it. An assumption that is far from the truth.

Unless we have a visual impairment, during every moment of our waking hours we look and see. But, as professionals, we need to learn how to observe in a range of situations.

This book's starting point is that observation is a powerful way of improving individual and collective classroom practice, but in order to be effective it must be carried out systematically and with rigour. A common reaction to the introduction of systematic observation is that, in the hurly-burly of school life, there 'just isn't time!' In the following chapters it is argued that systematic observation enables professionals to make better use of their time and that the rich data obtained is a reward for time well spent.

Throughout, the book focuses on work with children with special educational needs and their teachers, and reflects my experience and expertise in special education. In some cases I have deliberately given examples of work with children and young people with profound and multiple learning difficulties in order to highlight their position on the special needs continuum. It must be stressed, however, that the principles identified are not restricted to those with special educational needs but can be applied to any learner, at any time, in any situation. The emphasis on the analytical tools and critical thinking used to reach an understanding of the relationship between teaching and learning is also carried forward into appraisal and self-assessment.

The book is in two sections. Part One deals with the theory of observation and includes a critical survey of its uses, techniques and strategies. The practical examples given in this section, particularly those in Chapter 3 *Recording Evidence*, are intended to provide the reader with ideas and insights which can be used creatively and flexibly in a variety of situations. The advantages and disadvantages of partnership-observation are discussed, and an example of such collaborative work is taken forward into Part Two, where Catherine Clark and Sally Leat consider the use of unstructured observation in a mainstream primary school with children who are at various stages of the Code of Practice (DfE 1994). Their work indicates some of the advantages of unstructured observation and illustrates that, with determination, every teacher can become an effective researcher.

Part Two continues with a wide range of practical examples of observation and John Harris considers how it can be used effectively to understand and to lessen the impact of the challenging behaviours of pupils. His work is firmly based on a study of children, with severe learning difficulties, whose challenging behaviours are often of such intensity, frequency and duration that they present the greatest test to their peers and their teachers. He identifies the close relationship between observation, interpretation and intervention.

John Moore's experience of working with teachers enables him to contextualise observation within the demands of professional development and appraisal. His chapter illustrates how appraisal through observation is a central part of a school's professional culture and his positive approach emphasises the importance of prizing and valuing the work of teachers in the classroom.

The central implication of the arguments put forward throughout the book are that a 'whole-school approach' is required in order to ensure that this powerful tool (observation) permeates all aspects of the work of a school. In building an *observing school*, the emphasis must always be on developing teachers' skills and it is my intention to encourage all who work with children and their teachers in *all* settings to develop those skills to the full and to contribute to the provision of a more effective education for every child. The book concludes, quite rightly I believe, with the possible ethical implications of observing others.

Finally, in order to avoid the irritating 'he/she' and 'him/he' and the possibly ungrammatical 'their', throughout the text I have used the terms 'she' for the teacher and 'he' for the pupil where relevant; no sexist implications are intended.

Acknowledgements

I would like to thank the following who, in one way or another, have helped and encouraged me during the writing of this book:

my co-authors and David Fulton
for their patience and support during two difficult years;

Lyn Layton and Richard Rose
for their careful and critical reading of individual chapters and for their invaluable comments and suggestions. Any shortcomings or inaccuracies, however, are my own;

Christopher Lockwood
for his willingness to share his insights into observation;

Noreen Stacey
who typed some of the manuscript and who never failed to respond to my cries for help;

my husband, **Philip**
for his support and for his consistent belief in me and my work;

the late **Professor Ron Gulliford**
who 'opened my eyes';

Dr Pat Ashton
who 'taught me to see'.

I am also grateful to the following for permission to reproduce figures or tables:
Frank Steel and David Fulton (Figure 1.1);
Alan Peacock and Routledge Publishers (Figure 1.3);
John Harris, Dave Hewett and BILD Publications (Table 2.2);
Harry Ayers *et al.* and David Fulton (Table 3.4).

Christina Tilstone
Birmingham
March 1998

Contributors

Catherine Clark is a lecturer in Education at Newcastle University where she teaches courses on 'special educational needs', 'the education of more able pupils' and 'professional development' for experienced teachers. She also works closely with teacher organisations in the UK including NASEN (National Association for Special Educational Needs) and NACE (National Association for Able Children in Education).

Her research interests include the concept of individual differences and its implications for teachers and pupils in ordinary schools, and innovative approaches to professional development utilising teacher research. Her publications are wide-ranging and her most recent include *New Directions in Special Needs* (Cassell 1997) with Alan Dyson, Alan Millward and David Skidmore; *Theorising Special Education* (Routledge 1998) with Dyson and Millward; and, in the field of 'more able education', *Educating Able Children: Resource Issues and Processes for Teachers* (David Fulton 1998), with Ralph Callow.

John Harris obtained a degree in Psychology at the University of Swansea and went on to the University of Nottingham where he was awarded an MA in Child Development and a PhD for research on early language development. He is also a registered clinical psychologist. Following a brief spell at Trent Polytechnic, he was appointed lecturer in the School of Education at the University of Cardiff. From 1987–8 he was psychological consultant for the City of Hamilton, Ontario and Visiting Associate Professor at McMaster University. Since 1990 he has been Chief Executive of the British Institute of Learning Disabilities where he has continued to expand his research interests.

His wide range of publications include *Early Language Development: Implications for Clinical and Educational Practice* (Routledge 1990) and *Innovations in Educating Children with Severe Learning Difficulties* (Lisieux Hall 1993) and a number of books, training manuals and independent study units for BILD Publications. He is an honorary research fellow in the School of Education, University of Birmingham and a member of the editorial boards of *The Journal of Applied Research in Intellectual Disability* and the *British Journal of Learning Disabilities*.

Sally Leat's first degree was a BSc in Geography, after which she obtained a PGCE in primary education. Her first teaching post was in Cornwall and, following a long career break to start a family, she returned to part-time teaching as a learning support teacher. Her Master's degree included courses in special needs and her dissertation focused on the role of observation in the identification of children with learning difficulties.

She is now a learning support/special needs teacher working in primary schools in the North East of England with children with a variety of special educational needs including global difficulties, dyslexia, cerebral palsy and speech and behaviour problems. Her responsibilities include close liaison with class teachers and SENCOs (Special Educational Needs Coordinators) to devise and implement IEPs (Individual Education Plans) with a particular emphasis on language, literacy and numeracy targets.

John Moore was recently appointed Principal Adviser to the new Kent LEA, with special responsibility for Kent's strategy for meeting special educational needs, following service with Kent County Council as Inspector and then Senior Adviser and Commissioner for SEN (Special Educational Needs). He previously held posts in primary, secondary and special schools and as a Senior Lecturer in Special Education at Oxford Polytechnic.

He has worked for the Services' Children's Education Authority, acting as a consultant on the management of special educational needs in mainstream schools with a particular focus on differentiation, and is a regular contributor to conferences and university courses throughout the UK. He has also published widely on the role of the LEA in meeting special educational needs.

In 1993 he was elected to the Editorial Board for NASEN Journals and also gave evidence to the House of Commons Select Committee dealing with Statements and Provision. He is now a member of the National Policy Forum for SEN, funded by the Education and Social Research Council and a council member of the National Association of Advisory Officers for Special Education.

Christina Tilstone has taught children with learning difficulties in a variety of settings and since 1983 has worked in teacher education. After completing an Open University distance learning course, she went on to gain an advanced diploma and one of her Masters' degrees in Special Education at the University of Birmingham; her second higher degree was in Teacher Education at the University of Leicester; and her PhD was from the University of Birmingham.

She is now a Senior Lecturer in Special Education at the University of Birmingham, and is responsible for the coordination of the Learning Difficulties (Distance Education) Course. She has published widely on aspects of teaching children with severe learning difficulties and is currently Editor of the *British Journal of Special Education*, a leading UK special needs journal. Her research interests are in curriculum design and development in schools providing for pupils with severe and moderate learning difficulties, and in the ongoing professional development of their teachers by distance education.

PART ONE

Chapter 1

The Value of Observation

Christina Tilstone

'Observation' is a term commonly used by all who work with children and young people, particularly with those with special educational needs. It is a word that rolls off the tongue and is assumed to have a generally accepted meaning, like 'interaction' or 'cooperation', although, like these terms, it is open to a wide range of interpretations. Its connotations may vary in intensity and complexity and range from implications of analysis ('scrutinising' or 'investigating') to the more informal: 'looking' or 'glancing'. By far the most common definition offered by professionals working with children with special educational needs is 'watching', but watching, without analysis or interpretation, is of little value.

The many agencies and individuals, involved in the care and education of a child with educational needs will undoubtedly use some form of observation in their work. Figure 1.1, devised by Steel (1991), is a useful reminder of the range of professionals who may be responsible for meeting the needs of any child; the list is by no means exhaustive.

To professionals, observation is vital for a variety of reasons, and Figure 1.2 illustrates ways in which it is used by staff in a special school working with a range of children with special educational needs. The list is not definitive and in particular contexts its form and purpose will depend on the nature and severity of the needs of individual children, and on the training and experience of the professionals involved.

The list indicates the value of the skills of observation in the identification of the needs of children, in extending their experiences, and in facilitating their learning. Why then is so little time and attention given to their acquisition?

1

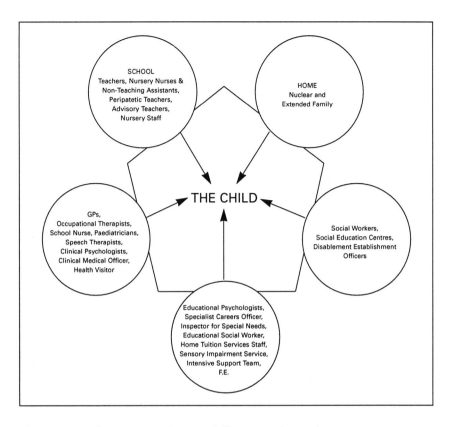

Figure 1.1 Influences on the pupil (from Steel 1991)

Undervalued and underestimated skills and competencies

Some people may acquire basic observation skills with little effort, but most professionals need some form of training. If, as with many aspects of professional practice, observation has to be *taught* not *caught*, why is it not a prominent part of training and professional development courses? Although students on initial teacher education courses spend at least 60 per cent of their time in schools acquiring teaching skills by what Stones and Morris (1972) describe as 'sitting next to Nellie', the art of accurate observation is seldom included in their syllabuses. Wragg is amongst the writers and researchers who have consistently stressed its importance (1994; 1993; 1984; 1979) and consequently some primary initial teacher training courses of three or four years duration are beginning to include it as a discrete element. It is, however, rarely considered on one year, primary level PGCE (Postgraduate Certificate of Education) courses, and

- *For the assessment of:*
  - knowledge, understanding and skills in all areas of the curriculum;
  - ability in all areas of development (physical, emotional, social and cognitive);
  - approaches to problem-solving;
  - behaviour;
  - vision;
  - hearing;
  - reactions to stimuli;
  - appropriate rewards (for children who find choice difficult);
  - methods of communication and interaction;
  - cultural similarities and differences.

- *For the monitoring of:*
  - individual pupil progress;
  - levels of concentration;
  - patterns of learning;
  - mismatch between learning opportunities and the experiences offered;
  - health problems;
  - the effects of medication;
  - the effects of the general classroom environment (especially visual stimuli and noise levels for children with sensory impairments);
  - the effectiveness of
    intervention programmes,
    teaching methods,
    grouping for learning,
    equipment and materials.

- *For the development of:*
  - whole-school policies;
  - the curriculum;
  - greater professional competence.

- *For the evaluation of:*
  - curriculum content in relation to need;
  - teaching;
  - school organisational structures;
  - policies;
  - resources.

- *For general information on:*
  - how children develop;
  - friendships;
  - interests and hobbies;
  - family relationships;
  - a greater understanding of a child's point of view.

Figure 1.2 The uses of observation

even less on those for secondary teacher training. Established teachers on in-service courses fare no better and, in a recent discussion with a large group of students from various parts of the UK, it was disconcerting to discover that only one school had made observation a focus for INSET (in-service education and training). Even then, it was not included as a topic in its own right, but as part of a day devoted to an examination of the challenging behaviour of pupils. A major report (SENTC 1996) which addressed key issues in initial teacher training and the continuing professional development of teachers, with responsibility for children with special educational needs, contains full lists of competencies produced by twelve monitoring groups covering areas such as 'Learning Support'; 'Autism'; 'Specific Learning Difficulties'; and 'Visual and Hearing Impairments'. Although all twelve emphasised that teachers should have the knowledge and the skills to be able to identify, assess, monitor and evaluate in a range of situations, observation was only specifically mentioned by three groups; two in the context of recording systems and one in terms of child development.

In contrast, nursery nurse training includes observation as part of the child care syllabus, and portfolios of observations are required for NVQ (National Vocational Qualification) awards. In social work training, however, Fawcett (1996) comments that other demanding priorities have forced observation out of the courses, although there is some evidence that the recent emphasis on child abuse has re-established child observation on courses recognised by CCETSW (Central Council for Education and Training of Social Workers).

Ideally, professional development courses should be designed to encourage groups of professionals from complementary disciplines to work collaboratively. Lacey and Lomas (1993) offer examples of syllabuses and the recommended training methods for such courses, including joint problem-solving and decision-making. Nevertheless innovatory practices are taking place in some areas only as a consequence of the vision and determination of individual educators, rather than as a result of Government initiatives. The Government's Green Paper, *Excellence for All Children: Meeting Special Educational Needs* (DfEE 1997) does, however, stress the need for collaborative working in the context of inclusion although, unfortunately, it gives no explanation of how 'working together' will be achieved. There is an implicit assumption that, through the process of striving for inclusive practices, a critical examination of the roles of individuals will emerge and a more coherent and cohesive approach to meeting the needs of children with special educational needs will result. It must, however, be recognised that an emphasis on the ideology of collaborative work does not produce a clear definition of its meaning and does not provide information on the necessary skills (including observation) which are central to multi-disciplinary work with children.

The inherent difficulties of multidisciplinary teams have been closely examined, both in the literature (Lacey and Lomas 1993; Orelove and Sobsey 1991; Maychell and Bradley 1991; Steel 1991) and through other government reports and circulars (for example, HMI 1991). Issues such as the lack of clearly defined roles, poorly coordinated working practices and inadequate communication have been identified as major stumbling blocks to collaborative work. If the different interpretations of the tools of observation are added to these areas of potential conflict, the needs of individual children are even less likely to be adequately met.

Common understanding

As professionals tend to interpret the meaning of observation in many different ways, its use as a means of obtaining information is often limited. Although observation is not an end in itself, but a process which leads to critical investigation, there is a tendency, unfortunately, to regard it as a marginal activity only used to confirm prejudices. A teacher who commented that the 'vicious little thug is always head-butting other children' had in fact only seen the child engage in an activity which could loosely be termed 'head-butting' once during a two week period, but her *observation* ensured that her jaundiced view was endorsed. Another member of staff may well have observed that 'he is a high-spirited youngster anxious to play with friends'.

As previously stated, the most common definition of observation is the 'act of watching'. Through his observational studies of human behaviour, Desmond Morris, the zoologist, has popularised and legitimised the art of 'people watching' (Morris 1977; 1985; 1991; 1994). He attempts to be objective and to avoid the natural prejudices which tend to colour our judgements. As he explains in *The Human Animal: a Personal View of the Human Species* (1994):

> My method, like that of any other field naturalist, is that of the observer. I am a watcher rather than an experimenter. I use my trained eye to see, as clearly as possible, the patterns of human activity...if I succeed I will lead you into the centre of the human arena as an invisible witness, able to watch the events unfold there as if seeing

them for the very first time. The most ordinary and commonplace will, I hope, be revealed as subtle and fascinating; the most bizarre and obscure as suddenly understandable.

(p.7)

Watching others is a commonplace, social behaviour, often undertaken surreptitiously or sometimes more openly if the observer feels that he or she is not being noticed. Classic people watchers (net-curtain twitchers!) watch their neighbours' comings and goings and then make judgements on what they see. The art is to carry out the activity in secret which gives it an air of excitement and impropriety; a feeling of 'naughty but nice'. The observers may be heard to whisper 'I told you so', and sometimes, 'Well I never!' when something unpredictable has been noted. We watch our favourite football team or television programme openly but still, in similar ways, pass judgements which are usually determined by our prejudices and mindsets and are, therefore, totally predictable. As Fawcett (1996) reminds us: '... we have a tendency to see what we are looking for and to look for only what we know about' (p.3). A frightening prospect, as members of the team may not share a common interpretation of observation and may only see actions which fuel their own beliefs and opinions. Thus, subjective opinions may be perpetuated, leading to an inaccurate and damaging assessment of a child's abilities and potential.

Defining observation

If the skill of observation has such relevance, it is important to find a working definition which will promote a common understanding of its practical value, but at the same time acknowledge its limitations. Some degree of subjectivity is unavoidable, but it is important to lessen the effect. Boehm and Weinberg (1997) comment that the level of precision with which one observes is influenced by the needs, interests, and experience of the observer. As Clark and Leat argue in Chapter 5, much of what we see is the result of casual, non-directed activity and is often unstructured. In order to make sense of observations, whether structured or unstructured, they must be carried out systematically. I therefore suggest the following working definition:

The systematic, and as accurate as possible, collection of usually visual evidence, leading to informed judgements and to necessary changes to accepted practices.

Professional roles and expectations

Professionals working with children and young people in an educational context will regularly engage in a wide range of activities. As early as 1968, Jackson estimated that, in a mainstream classroom, teachers were involved with pupils in the following ways:

- giving information;
- making suggestions;
- requesting;
- reprimanding;
- praising;
- greeting;
- answering questions.

He stated that, through these activities, teachers participated each day in over 1,000 interpersonal exchanges with pupils. His research was carried out before the influence of the Warnock Report (DES 1978) on the integration of children with special educational needs into mainstream schools, and the subsequent *1981 Education Act* which declared that an ordinary school should be the normal place for the education of children with SEN (special educational needs); an ideal developed further in the Green Paper (DfEE 1997) with a thrust for the creation of inclusive schools which would lay the foundations for an inclusive society.

In 1968 when Jackson reported his findings, a proportion of children were thought to be ineducable and were excluded from the education system. Children with severe learning difficulties were considered to have intellectual, emotional and social problems of such severity that they were cared for by Health personnel in occupation centres, training centres or long-stay hospitals. In 1971 the *Education (Handicapped Children) Act* was passed and responsibility for these children was transferred from health authorities to local education authorities when it was at last recognised that there were not two sorts of children (those who are handicapped and those who are not) and that all children have a basic right to education. As many of these children are now educated in mainstream schools (as are other children with SEN), the following can be added to Jackson's list:

- exchanging information;
- using non-verbal communication;
- differentiating;
- counselling;

7

- facilitating;
- empowering.

All exchanges rely on teachers watching pupils and making snap judgements in order to develop or end interactions. Such judgements are not usually the product of systematic observation, but the result of brief scans of the classroom. Studies of teacher behaviour have shown that teachers frequently misinterpret interpersonal exchanges and instigate wrong or different interactions to those normally expected. Good and Brophy (1978) emphasise that past experiences, biases and prejudices can lead to inaccurate interpretations of what is actually happening, and stress that it is all too easy to fall into the trap of expecting a pupil to behave in a certain way or to make predictions and inferences based on scanty evidence. Sharman, Cross and Vennis (1995) stress the importance of avoiding judgements based on single observations, which they consider to be like snapshots. Although the camera may not lie, in their view it can often distort. The following example is taken from an Open University in-service pack designed to improve teachers' observation skills for curriculum evaluation (Ashton *et al*. 1980).

> Sometimes though, inferences are drawn from inadequate evidence which means there is a possibility that they are incorrect or unsubstantiated. For example, all the pupils who put up their hand in response to a question may know the answer. However, some of them may not in fact know, but they have discovered that raising a hand when everyone else does is a way of avoiding the teacher's attention. The evidence in this instance is not sufficient to support the teacher's inference, which is therefore unsubstantiated and, as such, is a very dubious base for future action.
>
> (Block 2 *The pupils and the curriculum*, p.14)

Easen *et al*. (1992) provide a fascinating example, from a residential home for children with disabilities, of incorrect judgements made on scant evidence. Gleason was watching two boys with profound and multiple learning disabilities (lying on two parallel mats during a rest period) use two toy lawnmowers in purposeful and intentional cooperative play. They began by rolling around the mats using their limited movement to push the lawnmowers towards each other. In the first instance, they appeared to be intent on exchanging them, but suddenly the game changed direction and each boy tried to take the other's mower while guarding his own; later they returned to an exchange of mowers:

> Thomas grabs hold of the approaching lawnmower and pushes it into Danial's chest. Each boy relinquishes his lawnmower in the space

between them. Thomas moves closer to the toys, picks up the white-handled lawnmower and pushes it into Danial's stomach. After the jab, he picks it up and swings it over Danial's head. It wavers and falls close to Danial, but never touches his head. Danial does not reach for the toy over his head, but for the blue-handled toy in front of him. He pushes it towards Thomas. With this, Thomas withdraws the white handled toy from over Danial's head.

(p.322)

At this time, a member of staff entered the room. She looked at the boys and reprimanded both of them for fighting. She then moved them and the mats away from each other. Their activities stopped. Her interpretation of their actions as 'a fight' took a split second, but the evidence from Gleason's sustained observations showed a sophisticated level of co-operative play.

Expecting specific behaviours from pupils can make professionals themselves behave in a particular way which will, in turn, shape the children's responses to the situation. The following example resulted in unnecessary labelling and stereotyping.

John

The teacher thought that John was lazy because, in her view, he did not concentrate when she asked him a question. He frequently gave the wrong answer and she criticised him each time he did so. John started to avoid the teacher, and completed less and less work, which reinforced the teacher's predictions of laziness. John was constantly being reprimanded and made as little contact with her as possible. She interpreted his actions as non-compliance, and through the continual use of the words 'naughty' and 'difficult' in the staffroom, John was labelled as a 'disruptive pupil' throughout the school. John's label brought with it low expectations on the part of other staff, and the consequent feedback had a significant effect on John's performance and on his self-esteem. The staff began to expect less and less from him and the cycle continued: low expectations became self-fulfilling prophecies. Finally, John started to truant and the educational psychologist was called in. He continuously observed John in a range of activities and discovered that the pupil had some difficulties in responding in certain conditions. A hearing loss was suspected, which was later confirmed.

Labelling and stereotyping pose a major challenge in education, and can be the result of an inadequate definition of the term 'special educational needs'. Professionals may use labels such as 'learning difficulties' or 'autism' as shorthand to identify characteristics and to obtain resources, but once given, a label assigns its bearer to a group of similarly labelled individuals. Booth (1985) uses Down's syndrome as an example. Although the syndrome is a chromosomal abnormality, the term, he states, is used to refer to the 'physical signs of the impairments' which it may produce. Thus two assumptions are made: firstly that everyone with Down's syndrome has exactly the same impairments; secondly that Down's syndrome defines the common physical, intellectual and emotional features of a group of people with trisomy, consequently the clinical description becomes an inaccurate stereotype. Thus one defect may be used to indicate a whole personality or identity. John's teacher is not alone in making assumptions based solely on expectations.

Jackson (1968) also questions the training of professionals working with children, and suggests that although it is assumed that they watch children in order to improve learning and the quality of life, they rarely have time to see *how* the children are actually responding to the intervention or to the situation which they, the professionals, have planned. For example, many teachers, Jackson argued, are considered to be primarily 'activity managers', who decide on and provide a set of activities which they believe will further their pupils' knowledge and keep them engaged. He emphasised that although the ultimate aim of teaching is to enable pupils to learn, often a teacher's immediate preoccupation is to get pupils to participate in, and maintain, a set of activities.

Professionals as theorisers

In addition, and often as a result of their role as activity managers, teachers, along with other professionals, are also 'practical theorisers'. Teaching is a fluid activity which is constantly changing and each teacher makes sense of it by building up personal theories of what 'works', which then become the basis for subsequent teaching. Such theories are rarely articulated and remain unchallenged. They become part of the folklore of teaching, and were referred to by Ashton, Henderson, Merritt and Mortimer (1983) as 'implicit theorising'. 'Explicit theorising', on the other hand, employs methods of enquiry in order to heighten awareness, formulate ideas, and to test beliefs and assumptions. Explicit theorising, therefore, is a public, intellectual process which is open to scrutiny and debate, and is not concerned with the private acquisition of knowledge. Figure 1.3 illustrates the concept of the teacher as a practical theoriser and, although it is concerned with *classroom* practice, the model has applications in many other settings. Theorising is regarded as a familiar activity in which all professionals engage and which is not considered to be an optional exercise.

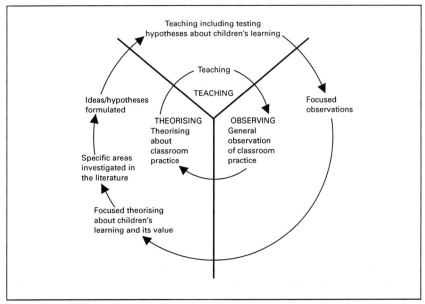

Figure 1.3 The observation-theorising-teaching cycle (from Ashton *et al.* 1989)

The inner circle represents the usual practice in the classroom, where teachers make *unsystematic observations* and use them to generate implicit theories on which their subsequent teaching will be based. For example, a teacher notes that a child has finished a task quickly, and may consequently *theorise* that he is the brightest in the class, the most interested, or has worked inaccurately and superficially. The teacher's next actions will be based on this implicit *theory* and she may, for example, give the child more demanding or more detailed work.

The second circle illustrates unfocused or unstructured observation which uses subjective impressions as a starting point for flexible data gathering and allows the unexpected and surprising to be taken into account. Sharman, Cross and Vennis (1995) point out that this type of observation is usually triggered as the result of interesting or unexpected events. The results can provide a holistic view of the child, which is valuable in itself or can lead to the pinpointing of a problem, focus or issue, requiring in-depth analysis. Unfocused or unstructured observation is explained in detail in Chapter 5.

The outer circle illustrates *focused observation*. Subjective impressions are also used as a starting point for objective data gathering, leading to the generation of a theory on more substantial evidence, which, in turn, encourages the testing of ideas and assumptions through teaching and further observation (Ashton, Henderson and Peacock 1989; Peacock and Tilstone 1991).

The processes involved in the second and outer circles prevent superficial theorising and possible decisions made on the basis of insufficient evidence. Systematic observation, either structured or unstructured, encourages the categorisation and analysis of data, the re-examination of ideas and the search for a better understanding of pupils within the context of the classroom or school in order that learning, in the widest sense of the word, can be improved.

Action research

The view of systematic observation put forward in this book has much in common with *action research* in that its central emphasis is on practitioners making systematic studies of their work practices as a means of achieving more securely founded actions, which in turn give rise to further enquiry (Ashton, Henderson and Peacock 1989). Webb (1990) explores the different ways in which researchers within the disciplines of sociology, psychology and pedagogy have sought to involve teachers in research, and identifies the diverse strands of the teacher-researcher movement. Her view of what she identifies as pedagogic research '... employs methods of enquiry, ways of presenting findings and publication outlets that are eclectic, pragmatic and readily accessible to teachers.' (p.3)

Stenhouse, whose work on the Humanities Curriculum Project (1975) increased the credibility of the action research movement, used action research to encourage the professional development of teachers through self-study and reflection. Thus, his emphasis was on internal initiation and embedded in his work is the idea of the 'reflective teacher practitioner'. Other authors use different terms: Vulliamy and Webb (1992), for example, use 'teacher as researcher' and Easen (1985) refers to the 'reflecting teacher', who, in his view, constantly strives to create an inner dialogue, concerned with all aspects of school-work, based on observation, reflection and consequent action. The reflecting teacher will consequently tend to select elements which are currently interesting or important and will exclude the rest. Additional elements may be considered at a later stage, as the nature of the focus shifts and changes.

Appraisal

The professionals involved in the education of children and young people with SEN are the *ultimate factor* in determining the quality of what goes on in the classroom or workplace and it is, therefore, important to consider the place of appraisal in the development of the professional skills necessary to improve teaching and learning. Moore, in Chapter 7, considers observation as a crucial part of the appraisal system and examines the concerns which surround the task of observing other colleagues. As Jones (1993) points out:

> Classroom observation is only one way of gathering data for appraisal purposes but if appraisal of performance is about improving the quality of children's education by improving teacher effectiveness, then looking at what is actually happening within the classroom is vital.

(p.67)

The foci on evidence, accurate description, reflection and change are as applicable to professional development as they are to practice in both the school and workplace. Observation for appraisal, as with observation for other purposes, is concerned with the making of judgements. These require the same techniques and strategies which facilitate children's learning, and the same emphasis on explicit criteria and record keeping. Lessons learned will only be effective if the atmosphere for observation is positive and supportive and based on mutual trust. Such issues are the basis of the following chapters. Professionals who are already using observation for purposes other than appraisal will appreciate its value and power.

References

Ashton, P. M. E., Henderson, E. S., Merritt, J. E. and Mortimer, D. J. (1983) *Teacher Education in the Classroom: Initial and In-Service*. London: Croom Helm.

Ashton, P. M. E., Henderson, E. S., Peacock, A. (1989) *Teacher Evaluation through Classroom Evaluation: the Principles and Practice of IT-INSET*. London: Routledge.

Ashton, P. M. E., Hunt,P., Jones, S. and Watson, G. (1980) *Curriculum in Action: an Approach to Evaluation*. Milton Keynes: Open University Press.

Biott, C. and Easen, P. (1994) *Collaborative Learning in Staffrooms and Classrooms*. London: David Fulton Publishers.

Booth, T. (1985) 'Labels and their consequences', in Lane, D. and Stratford, B. (eds) *Current Approaches to Down's Syndrome*. London: Holt, Rinehart and Winston.

Department for Education and Employment (1997) *Excellence for All Children: Meeting Special Educational Needs*. London: DfEE.

Department of Education and Science (1978) *Special Educational Needs: Report of the Committee of Enquiry into the Education of Handicapped Children and Young People* (The Warnock Report). London: HMSO.

Easen, P. (1985) *Making School-centred INSET Work*. London: The Open University in association with Croom Helm.

Easen, P., Gleason, J. J., Hull, R. and Pye, J. (1992) 'Close observation', in Booth, T., Swann, W., Masterton, M. and Potts, P. (eds) *Learning for All–1: Curricula for Diversity in Education*. London: Routledge.

Fawcett, M. (1996) *Learning Through Child Observation*. London: Jessica Kingsley.

Good, T. L. and Brophy, J. E. (1978) *Looking in Classrooms*, 2nd edn. London: Harper Row.

Her Majesty's Inspectorate (1991) *Interdisciplinary Support for Young Children with Special Educational Needs*. London: DES.

Jackson, P. W. (1968) *Life in Classrooms*. New York: Holt, Rinehart and Winston.

Jones, J. (1993) *Appraisal and Staff Development in Schools*. London: David Fulton Publishers.

Lacey, P. and Lomas, J. (1993) *Support Services and the Curriculum: a Practical Guide to Collaboration*. London: David Fulton Publishers.

Maychell, K. and Bradley, J. (1991) *Preparing for Partnership: Multi-agency Support for Special Needs*. Slough: NFER.

Morris, D. (1977) *Manwatching: a Field Guide to Human Behaviour*. London: Jonathan Cape.

Morris, D. (1985) *Bodywatching: a Field Guide to the Human Species*. London: Jonathan Cape.

Morris, D. (1991) *Babywatching*. London: Jonathan Cape.

Morris, D. (1994) *The Human Animal: a Personal View of the Human Species*. London: BBC Books.

Orelove, F. and Sobsey, D. (1991) *Educating Children with Multiple Disabilities: a Transdisciplinary Approach*. Baltimore: Paul Brookes.

Peacock, A. and Tilstone, C. (1991) 'IT-INSET and special education', in Upton, G. (ed.) *Staff Training and Special Educational Needs*. London: David Fulton Publishers.

SENTC (1996) *Professional Development to Meet Special Educational Needs* (Report to the Department of Education and Employment). London: SENTC.

Sharman, C., Cross, W. and Vennis, D. (1995) *Observing Children: a Practical Guide*. London: Cassells.

Steel, F. (1991) 'Working collaboratively within a multidisciplinary framework', in Tilstone, C. (ed.) *Teaching Pupils with Severe Learning Difficulties: Practical Approaches*. London: David Fulton Publishers.

Stenhouse, L. (1975) *An Introduction to Curriculum Research and Development*. London: Heinemann Educational.

Stones, E. and Morris, S. (1972) *Teaching Practice: Problems and Perspectives*. London: Methuen.

Vulliamy, G. and Webb, R. (eds) (1992) *Teacher Research and Special Educational Needs*. London: David Fulton Publishers.

Webb, R. (1990) *Practitioner Research in the Primary School*. London: Falmer Press.

Wragg, E. C. (1979) 'Interaction analysis as a feedback system for student teachers', in Bennett, N. and McNamara, D. (eds) *Focus on Teaching: Readings in the Observation and Conceptualisation of Teaching*. London: Longmans.

Wragg, E. C. (1984) (ed.) *Classroom Teaching Skills*. London: Croom Helm.

Wragg, E. C. (1993) *Primary Teaching Skills*. London: Routledge.

Chapter 2

The Techniques of Observation

Christina Tilstone

Although the main aim of this chapter is to review ways in which data is collected, it is important first to clarify the use of the terms 'techniques' and 'strategies', the meanings of which, like 'observation' itself, tend to vary from context to context. In this book the following meanings are recognised:

- *Techniques* sampling systems used in the collection of evidence, including continuous recording, and event- and time-recording;
- *Strategies* the means by which the information will be recorded (checklists, diaries, field notes, and schedules).

(adapted from Walker 1990)

Techniques and methods will be chosen according to the reasons for carrying out the observation. Cohen, Stern and Balaban (1997), in discussing the principles of observation suggest that in order to understand *any* child we are unravelling a mystery through observation, investigation and the recording of clues. If we reflect upon the apparent complexities of many children's special educational needs and consider the reasons given for observation by the staff from a variety of special schools in Chapter 1 (Figure 1.2), we are uncovering a mystery, and a very exciting one at that.

Observational techniques are often linked to large-scale quantitative and qualitative methods of research; a far cry from exploring the teaching and learning of children and young people in the classroom or workplace. Wragg (1994) reminds us that we are wrong to dismiss the use of such methods as being irrelevant to these settings. Unfortunately, however, quantitative methods evoke thoughts of the distribution, coding and analysis of hundreds of questionnaires or interviews in order to discover, for example, how many primary schools in England and Wales had a

SENCO (Special Educational Needs Coordinator) in place three months after the implementation of the *Code of Practice* (DfE 1994). He suggests that there are numerous times when professionals who deal with children and young people may need to know about the quantity of outcomes. It may be on a macro-school level of how many times in a week every pupil has access to a computer, or each client at a day centre has the opportunity to shop, or, at the micro-classroom level, of how many times a specific piece of software is used in a particular setting, or whether each young person is familiar with local or supermarket shopping. On the other hand, qualitative methods of research provide descriptions and accounts of events which take place in their natural settings and do not, in the main, conjure up such preconceived ideas. All professionals will recognise the need to observe, for example, the changing patterns of behaviour of one child or adult, or the way in which, over a period of time, he relates to a range of other people. The influences on qualitative methods are wide-ranging, and Wragg (1994) pays tribute to two traditions:

- cultural and social anthropology (for ethnographic observation);
- ethnology (for the study of patterns of animal behaviour).

Both rely on the collection of data which does not involve the use of a laboratory and both are at odds with the child psychologists of the nineteenth century who established child study centres (often at universities) in order to ensure that children could be observed in controlled surroundings. The exploration of qualitative methods has led to an ecological approach to the collection of data which takes into account not only what the child does, but also his environment; the location; the presence of others; and the rules and conditions which govern the situation.

Traditional educational researchers sometimes use other frameworks to describe research methods. Brause and Mayher (1991), for example, define research as 'hypothesis testing' or 'hypothesis generating'. Hypothesis testing is, in their view, the process of assessing or testing the validity of an existing, explicit theory. By using identified techniques, specific data is gathered which tests the accuracy or predictability of the child's learning or behaviour within the relevant setting. As such, hypothesis testing can be thought of in terms of *exploring* the *product*.

On the other hand, the authors define hypothesis generating research as 'an examination of a process', leading to the generation of a theory. Hypothesis generating studies start with an initial general premise, which is subject to scrutiny, and result in the narrowing and refining of the focus. Brause and Mayher (1991) state:

We may compare hypothesis generating research to investigative reporting in journalism, wherein the reporter checks out numerous leads hoping one will lead to fruitful information. The reporter collects all available data, sifting through it to develop a theory which accounts for and predicts events.

(p.54)

Table 2.1 indicates the differences between the two approaches.

Table 2.1 (adapted from Brause and Mayher 1991)

Hypothesis testing research

Origin	an explicit theory or set of beliefs, facts or assumptions
Process	deductive
Context	sometimes controlled, but can be in natural settings
Outcome	either support for, or the modification or the revision of, the theory

Hypothesis generating research

Origin	the identification of a phenomenon which is unpredictable
Process	inductive
Context	natural, spontaneous
Outcome	a tentative theory or hypothesis which may lead to further investigation

Depending upon the focus and context of the investigation, such distinctions can be beneficial in the search for a specific observational technique.

As Fawcett (1996) points out, observation has a long history and has not only been a central skill in the production of great art (from prehistoric times), but has been the basis of scientific discovery. It is also an essential tool in the study of child development which, historically, has had a radical influence on the techniques and methods used by all professionals working with children and young people, particularly those with special educational needs.

What prompts an investigation?

Figure 1.2 (in Chapter 1) shows why professionals working with children with special educational needs considered observation to be an important tool. The answers given were listed under the specific headings of:

- assessment;
- monitoring;

- development;
- evaluating;
- general information.

When the teachers were asked 'what prompted?' the need for an investigation they gave answers which were general in nature and fell under broader headings. Although these did not match precisely the five headings given above, each can be applied to the following:

- to follow up and make explicit an *internalised hunch*;
- to pinpoint a problem, issue or focus which may require more in-depth observation;
- to provide information on a pupil's learning processes;
- to become more aware of the effects of one's own teaching on pupils.

To follow up and make explicit an internalised hunch

In responding to the needs of children, we are constantly gaining fleeting impressions, which are fuelled by our intuition and become something much stronger: a hunch. Staffroom talk often includes such phrases as:

'Emily is crying a lot, do you think she is being bullied?'
'Rosa seems to be having more *petit mals*, I have a hunch that she isn't taking her medication.'
'Billy is playing up more than usual in maths, I wonder if he needs extra support?'

Such hunches are significant and, as responsive and responsible teachers, we need to investigate them.

Susan

Susan, aged 12, and with severe learning difficulties, seemed to be taking an inordinate amount of time to complete tasks that she had carried out relatively quickly in the past. She had always appeared a contented child who was pleasant and eager to please. She often articulated that she liked school and was enthusiastic about her work. The teacher was concerned that her 'sluggish behaviour', as she described it to her colleagues, could be due to an underlying medical or social problem.

- Was Susan getting enough sleep?
- Was she suffering from an undetected illness?
- Had her diet changed?

She had a hunch that something was wrong, or possibly that a set of circumstances had changed and, consequently, Susan's learning was suffering.

Susan was one of 14 pupils in her class, all of whom had worked with the teacher over a period of time. The OFSTED inspectors had commented, during a recent visit to the school, that the teaching of the group was effective in a wide variety of settings and that there was a cheerful, welcoming and purposeful atmosphere in the classroom. Part of the success of the teaching environment was due to the fact that the pupils knew exactly what was expected of them, and routines and ground rules were clear. The teacher prided herself on the predictable nature of the classroom. The beginnings and endings of lessons were clearly defined by set routines for each curriculum subject. As in many other special schools, the day started with a *greeting* time to allow the children to settle into the class.

She decided to observe Susan carrying out three routine tasks per day over one week:

- settling down during the greeting routine;
- starting work on the first curriculum subject of the day;
- preparing to go home.

Her records showed that, apart from preparing to go home, Susan was taking longer and longer on the other two tasks. In the first activity the time taken to take off her coat and seat herself increased over the week. In addition, the records showed that before starting work on the first curriculum subject she would look out of the window, talk to other pupils, sort and re-sort her materials. The teacher noted that she did not complain, and seemed her usual cheerful self, and therefore the idea that Susan might be ill, lacked supporting evidence. The teacher then observed Susan in a range of other activities and found that she was more enthusiastic when starting activities which she had chosen herself, and where she was encouraged to work independently.

The teacher now had other ideas, another *internalised hunch*, which needed testing. Was the teaching environment taxing enough for Susan or was she getting bored and *switching off*? Had the routines and rituals of the classroom become survival skills, rather than giving shape to the day and making it predictable, as the teacher thought? Sebba, Byers and Rose (1993) warn that such practices can turn into symbols of staff control over pupils and that they can become soothing for both pupils and staff. Was this the case with Susan?

Over the next few weeks Susan's teacher *tunnelled* into her assumptions, altered her routines, and used the opportunity to develop strategies which allowed Susan to manage her own time and to take more control over her own learning. Later records showed that her latter hunch was right. Her internalised hunch led to changes in the curriculum which, when fully established, benefited all pupils.

To pinpoint a problem issue or focus which may require more in-depth observation.

All teachers have a number of issues, topics or problems which they would like to explore in more depth. It may be a concern about an individual child; an aspect of the school day; or as in the example of Susan, a routine in the classroom. Like John, in Chapter 1, Harjinda had been labelled as disruptive.

Harjinda

Harjinda attends a unit for children with moderate learning difficulties within a large inner-city primary school. He is in Year 3 and although he and his peers started at the school together, he has no close friends. He enjoys the routine of the classroom and the school, and appears to accept the company of other children, and to be tolerated by them. Harjinda is the second generation of his family to be educated in his home town, and although English is the main language spoken at home, his own verbal skills are delayed. His receptive language is only slightly delayed and is on a par with most of the other children in the unit; his expressive language is a problem, for although he talks in sentences, he has a large tongue and his speech is often indistinct. He was Statemented in Year 1.

His behaviour in class is high-spirited but generally tolerated with good humour by his peers and the classroom staff. Nevertheless, complaints were continually being received about his bad behaviour outside the classroom, particularly at lunchtime. His teachers were surprised by the volume of complaints, and decided to try to pinpoint the problem. The SENCO observed him in the dining-room for three sessions over two weeks, and found that he spent the entire time isolated from his peers. The reasons given by the dinner ladies stemmed from incidents of disruptive behaviour at lunchtimes in the previous term; as a consequence he was routinely isolated from his peers and ate his lunch alone. This surprised the SENCO as many reports of bad behaviour had been received during this term when he was routinely isolated. She now had some evidence to indicate that there was a problem, albeit rather different from the one she had originally anticipated. She and the teacher decided to explore the issue in more depth and consequently set up a series of short, but systematic, observations in different contexts over a month. From the data gathered it was apparent that Harjinda demonstrated aggressive behaviour when others either misinterpreted his speech, or when his intentions were misunderstood. Such behaviour occurred more often at times when he mixed with those pupils and staff who normally had little contact with him. The aggressive attacks were most frequent in the playground, often when interacting with the dinner ladies.

As in the case of John (in Chapter 1), Harjinda had been labelled as a troublemaker by some staff, who had then segregated him at lunchtime, *in case* he misbehaved.

Three important strategies were employed as a result of this investigation:

- Harjinda was taught a basic signing system, which was not so taxing for him as the spoken word;
- all the staff and pupils were also taught Harjinda's system (mainly by him) which helped to raise his flagging self-esteem and confidence, but allowed him to have some control over the situation;
- all staff and pupils were encouraged to focus their attention on his positive behaviour and to praise it where appropriate.

This is not necessarily the end, for a critical evaluation of the new strategies is needed. Nevertheless, Harjinda now sits with his peers at lunchtime!

To provide information on how a pupil learns

Raban, Wells and Nash (1979) emphasise that education is not a continuous process, and is different for every child: 'Progress is uneven and particular events and experiences provide both points of departure for periods of rapid progress and stumbling blocks which may take some time to overcome' (p.58).

The fact that children learn in different ways, in different contexts and at different stages in their development, indicates the importance of observation. To observe and record how a pupil goes about a particular task will provide valuable information, on which future teaching can be based. Rather than giving an example, which only applies to one child, it will be more useful to consider a series of questions devised to discover ways in which all children with special educational needs approach learning. The work of Cohen, Stern and Balaban (1997) has been used as a starting point, but a limited number of general examples under a series of headings are given. Other general questions will need to be asked and, in addition, specific ones formulated in response to each child's needs, the curriculum content, and context in which he is being taught.

The setting
- What is happening around the pupil when he is engaged in the activity?
- Who are the nearby *significant* adults and peers?
- How are the pupils grouped for learning?

The stimulus
- How does the pupil use the materials for the set activity?
- What is the amount and kind of adult supervision?
- Does the pupil make generalisations (in other sessions or at other times) from using specific material?

Reactions to the task
- What is the length of concentration time on the specific task?
- Does the pupil show persistence in mastering the task?
- Does he show curiosity in any way?

Reactions to people
- How and with whom, does the pupil make most contact (adults and/or peers)?
- How does the pupil react to sharing an adult with others?
- How does he communicate?

Clues to cognitive functioning
- How does the pupil become involved in the learning experience?
- Does he show curiosity, if so, how?
- Does he seek help?

To become more aware of the effect of your own teaching on your pupils

From the examples given above, it will be seen that it is impossible to observe and to record learning without recognising its effect on teaching. The recordings made of Susan and John subsequently directly influenced future teaching. It was emphasised in Chapter 1 that all observers bring to all situations personal understanding and beliefs which are often not articulated and are rarely recognised. An important aspect of observation is to acknowledge, on the one hand that such biases exist; on the other, to make a conscious effort to record exactly what is seen. Reflecting on the data obtained will almost certainly help to challenge assumptions and lead to further questions which, in turn, will raise doubts on the certainty of the interpretations. The questions formulated by teachers observing children's responses to the curriculum (Ashton *et al.* 1980), are valuable when considering if the teaching is *right*:

- What might the children be learning from what they are doing which is different from what I intended?
- Do I value that learning?
- How worthwhile is the learning that I am trying to encourage?
- Am I really providing the children with opportunities to learn what I intended?
- What might I have done which provoked that response from children?

(p.7)

Systematic observation requires: practice; concentration; and an understanding of the advantages and disadvantages of the techniques and strategies available, together with the will to record accurately. McCormick and James (1983) and Delamont (1976), in appealing for as much intellectual and emotional detachment as possible, stress the need for what they term the 'familiar to become strange'. Questions such as those above, asked after the observation has taken place, may help. Focusing on taken-for-granted features of the classroom setting, such as a gender issue or the grouping of children, for a few minutes before attempting to record, may also help to challenge perceptions and conceptualisations.

Techniques

The choice of the appropriate technique will depend on the *focus* of the observation, i.e. whether the emphasis is on what has been learned; the *length* and *strength* of a particular behaviour (*the product*); or *how* the learning has taken place (*the process*). Some techniques are more applicable to either quantitative or qualitative approaches, although many are suitable for both and may often be used to complement each other.

Event recording (or frequency counts)

Event recording is often used when a professional, having pinpointed a specific problem or focus, needs to record the number of times a particular response is given by a child or group of children. Its roots stem from behaviour modification, particularly in operant condition studies when the observer records (using a simple tally system) the number of times a particular behaviour, such as pinching or head-butting, occurs before, during and after a programme of intervention. Children and young people with special educational needs often display a range of behaviours (interesting and challenging) which could be the focus of investigation, and it is vitally important to pinpoint the *exact* behaviour under scrutiny.

Jasmin

Jasmin is a pupil with a multisensory impairment who was considered by the multidisciplinary team to be 'excessively noisy'. 'Noisy' can of course mean anything from shuffling about to humming constantly, shouting out, giggling, talking loudly, or a combination of all of these behaviours, which Harris and Hewett (1996) would then label as 'big'. In Jasmin's case the 'small' (or exact) behaviour which was causing concern was an ear-piecing scream which she let out for no apparent reason at frequent intervals during the day. Despite its ferocity it was considered to be an expression of pleasure as she often smiled immediately afterwards and did not show any signs of distress. The problem was that the other pupils, all of whom had severe learning difficulties (including a few with some profound and multiple learning difficulties) were startled by her screams and their concentration was disrupted.

The initial recording of the screams took place over two days, but the results neither showed any recognisable pattern, nor threw any light on the reasons for the screaming: she screamed six times on one day; twice in the morning and four times in the afternoon; and three times the next day, all in the morning. Recording over a week, however, suggested that the screaming was linked to activity, as it always occurred at the start of an activity. Further investigation showed that the stimulus was the placing of hard objects in Jasmin's hands and she was immediately encouraged to use two hands to carry out the next step of the activity. Three responses from a long list were:

- cooking, in which she was encouraged to hold a spoon in one hand and a bowl in the other;

25

- music, in which she was encouraged to play a drum;
- personal and social education, in which she was encouraged to pour her own drink.

The records also confirmed that the scream probably indicated pleasure, and the staff concluded that:

- she had not anticipated the activity before feeling the object but she then linked the object with a pleasurable experience;
- all the activities that she was responding to involved senses other than touch (e.g. cooking smells, musical vibrations, the taste of drinks).

It was decided that more thought should be given to cueing her into activities through the use of *objects of reference* which allowed her to associate objects with the subsequent activities, all of which would have a sensory element: for example, the smell of chocolate for *cooking* and the feel of a vibrating guitar string for *music*. Taste proved a little difficult and, therefore, drink was linked to the *smell* of essential orange oil.

In addition, a programme to reward acceptable responses of pleasure was initiated and after four weeks the ear-piercing screams had been reduced to one or two per week!

In the example given above, the reason for the investigation was not only for Jasmin's benefit, but because her screams were causing problems for her peers. In a survey of why staff in special schools felt it necessary to change behaviours which challenge the system, Harris, Cook and Upton (1996) found that the disruption to others was as important a reason as injury to self or to others.

From clinical beginnings, this flexible technique has been adapted for use in a range of contexts. Teachers, for example, use event recording daily to monitor pupil absences (taking the register), and the only resources necessary to carry out the observations are pencil and paper. Ongoing classroom behaviours, such as the number of times pupils talk together or leave their seats without permission, can be recorded using these simple procedures. Hayes (1971) used pencil and paper to record the number of words a very underconfident child used when she spoke in a range of different situations. Turn-taking, at different times of the day, between pupils with severe learning difficulties has been recorded in a similar way (Tilstone 1991). More sophisticated equipment, such as wrist and digital counters, tally markers and clipboards, are often used in clinical studies and can also be helpful in the workplace. Wrist counters, in particular, avoid the inconvenience of carrying writing materials.

In the study of child development, event recording has taken on a very different meaning and has been used to describe a behavioural sequence in detail. Recording involves not only the frequency of occurrence of a particular behaviour, but a description of the unit of behaviour and the *events* surrounding it. Medinnus (1976) gives anger outbursts, fear reactions, quarrels, eating, and sympathetic responses as some of the behaviours studied using this technique. Recording involves the use of a traditional ABC Chart (Antecedent, Behaviour and Consequence); see Chapter 3.

An extension to event recording is what Wragg (1994) calls a 'critical event approach' in which:

> The observer looks for specific instances of classroom behaviour which are judged to be illuminative of some aspect of the teacher's style or strategies, an element of class management, for example, perhaps a rule being established, observed or broken, something which reflects interpersonal relationships or some other indicative event.
>
> (p.62)

Recording can be carried out on an adapted ABC Chart which can then be discussed with the children in order to obtain their perceptions.

Although event recording is an appropriate observational technique for a wide range of behaviours, it has obvious limitations. Hall, Hawkins and Axelrod (1975) emphasise that it is most appropriate for responses of a short duration which can be readily divided into single units. They give examples of its use in measuring the frequency of a shy pupil speaking, or an aggressive student making positive (rather than negative) comments, but they stress that the technique can have limitations when a behaviour cannot be defined precisely.

Duration recording

This technique is used to determine the length of actions or behaviours, and a stopwatch is often used for accuracy (Cartwright and Cartwright 1974). An infant teacher, for example, wishing to record the length of time a group of children played cooperatively in the *house-corner* without the intervention of an adult, would start the stopwatch as soon as the desired behaviour began. As with event recording, a precise description of the behaviour or action is necessary. For instance, does *cooperatively* mean sharing toys, talking to one another, or engaging in different activities alongside each other?

Observational techniques are of little value in themselves, and as was seen in the previous example of Jasmin, the interpretation (as objective as possible) of the recorded, factual, information is essential.

Recording Susan's behaviour

In a previous example, the length of time Susan took to complete three tasks was investigated. The technique used by the teacher to observe Susan's *sluggishness* was duration recording. Over a period of a week, she systematically observed and recorded each day, using a stopwatch, how long it took Susan to:

- settle down during the greeting routine;
- start work on the first curriculum subject of the day;
- prepare to go home.

As we have already seen, her findings confirmed her suspicions.

In considering the effectiveness of the technique, it is important to question whether an exact measurement of behaviours or actions is necessary. A major criticism may be that a concentrated effort is needed to obtain precise information, and that inaccurate records are obtained owing to other demands on the observer's time. Nevertheless, the data recorded is usually accurate enough to stimulate reflection and to effect useful changes in practice. In some situations, precise measurement can only be obtained by another member of staff acting as an observer, and partnerships in observation are discussed in detail in Chapter 4. The way in which the technique is used is largely determined by the focus of the observation and, in the previous example, it was possible for one person to use duration recording successfully over an extended period.

Recording intensity

A development of duration recording is *recording intensity*. Observing and recording the intensity of behaviour may be necessary in a range of situations, but particularly in dealing with challenging behaviour or in managing anger. It is an area where objectivity is impossible. Anxiety for example can be defined as 'a state of uneasiness' or 'a state of agitation' and, as has already been emphasised, observations will reflect egocentric and individual frames of reference. Harris and Hewett (1996) suggest that linking the target behaviour to other specific behaviours may help the observer to be as objective as possible. Although the next chapter deals specifically with recording observation, in order to illustrate the point, their example of a scale to measure behaviour which is considered 'excited' is given in Table 2.2.

Scale point 1 Simon sitting or standing and listening or speaking in an even voice.

Scale point 2 Simon speaking faster than usual and not waiting for others to reply.

Scale point 3 Simon speaking quickly and loudly; raising his hands or waving his arms.

Scale point 4 Simon shouting; waving arms and hands; repeatedly standing up and sitting down or (if standing) walking round.

Scale point 5 Simon running around shouting excitedly, waving arms and hands and not listening to anyone else.

Table 2.2 Scale to measure Simon's 'excited' behaviour (from Harris and Hewett 1996)

Time sampling, interval recording and continuous observation
Time sampling and *interval recording* are two other techniques which are particularly adaptable and can be used in a variety of ways.

Time sampling
Time sampling involves observing the pupil or pupils at the end of a pre-determined period, possibly every hour, and recording exactly what is happening. Yule (1987) suggests that precise timing is needed in order to avoid biased results. He gives the example of a nurse on a busy ward who is observing a patient every five minutes to see whether he or she is rocking or is engaged in some other self-stimulatory behaviour: 'Unless the nurse does look at exactly the end of the five minute interval, then she may find herself remembering to record only when she sees the patient engaged in the undesirable activity' (pp.19–20).

In this case, the technique was useful in revealing whether the behaviour was as problematic as was first thought. If the nurse recorded that the patient was rocking on the hour six or seven consecutive times, she would need to investigate the problem further. If, however, the rocking only occurred once during the six or seven occasions on which she recorded, perhaps it was not such a problem after all! Repeated (compared with random) observations will reveal the extent to which the behaviour is consistent.

Wragg (1994) uses time sampling (which he refers to as 'static sampling') rather differently in that observers build up a series of *snapshots* of a situation at regular intervals. Using the technique in this way, it is possible to take a small number of pupils and to build up a comprehensive picture of their activities over a period of time. As he points out, the major disadvantage of the method is that it is not possible to record a pattern or sequence of ongoing behaviours, and consequently the reciprocal nature of interactions is often lost and the data recorded seldom reveals cause and effect relationships. Time sampling may tell us *which* pupils are more helpful or aggressive than others, but it cannot tell us *why*. Fawcett (1996) warns of the temptation to carry on recording after the defined period, particularly if something interesting has happened. Individual techniques should not be seen in isolation and it is often desirable to use another technique to explore a behaviour highlighted by a previous one.

Interval recording

Interval recording requires a practitioner to estimate the total time she can devote to observation during the day, and to apportion it in equal parts. She may, for example, observe and record for five minutes every hour which would enable a stream of behaviours, actions or events to be recorded. Although some researchers (mainly those working on the modification of behaviour, such as Murphy and Goodhall 1980) regard interval recording as almost useless, it gives, however, an indication of both the frequency and duration of the actions, behaviours and events under scrutiny. As the method does not give *accurate* information, it is essential to realise that, although *indication* is the key word, its consciousness-raising function may prove invaluable for the busy practitioner.

Continuous observation

The most frequently used technique is *continuous recording*, which attempts to capture the full range, richness and complexity of the actions and behaviours of an individual child or of a group of children. It is useful in that, although time-consuming, it provides an excellent starting point for a more detailed enquiry and is an effective method of recording a stream of behaviours. It is obviously impossible to collect evidence in this way for a long period each day, but practitioners who use the technique regularly have reported that the quality of their recording has improved dramatically and that they have gained a greater understanding of their pupils.

During a ten minutes continuous recording, it is unlikely that you will have been able to record everything that a pupil does or says. Your recordings probably represent what has interested, excited or worried you most during the observation period. What do you think you have failed to notice? An impossible question, although asking it can prompt useful reflection (Ashton *et al.* 1980). In an attempt to respond, you may have discovered something about your own personal criteria which will have affected the selection and interpretation of your recording.

References

Brause, R. S. and Mayher, J. (1991) 'Research objectives: generating hypotheses, testing hypotheses and critiquing educational practice', in Brause, R. S. and Mayher, J. (eds) *Search and Re-search: What the Inquiring Teacher Needs to Know.* London: Falmer Press.

Cohen, D. H., Stern, V., Balaban, N. (1997) *Observing and Recording the Behaviour of Young Children.* New York: Teachers' College Press.

Cartwright, C. A. and Cartwright, C. P. (1974) *Developing Observation Skills.* London: McGraw.

Delamont, S. (1976) *Interaction in the Classroom.* London: Methuen.

Hall, R. V., Hawkins, R. P. and Axelrod, S. (1975) 'Measuring and recording student behaviour: a behaviour analysis approach,' in Weinberg, R. A. and Wood, F. H. (eds) *Observation of Pupils and Teachers in Mainstream and Special Education Settings: Alternative Strategies.* Minnesota: University of Minnesota.

Harris, J. and Hewett, D. (1996) 'Unit H: Strategies for observation and record keeping', in *Positive Approaches to Challenging Behaviours.* Kidderminster: BILD.

Hayes, J. E. (1971) 'The use of some contingency management techniques with a case of elective mutism', *School Applications of Learning Theory* 3, 34–9.

McCormick, J. and James, M. (1983) *Curriculum Evaluation in Schools*, 2nd edn. London: Croom Helm.

Medinnus, G. R. (1976) *Child Study and Observation Guide.* New York: John Wiley.

Murphy, G. and Goodhall, E. (1980) 'Measurement error in direct observation: a comparison of common recording methods', *Behaviour Research Therapy* 18, 147–50.

Raban, B., Wells, G. and Nash, T. (1979) 'Observing children learning to read', in Bennett, N. and McNamara, D. (eds) *Focus on Teaching: Readings in the Observation and Conceptualisation of Teaching.* London: Longman.

Sebba, J., Byers, R., Rose, R. (1993) *Redefining the Whole Curriculum for Pupils with Learning Difficulties.* London: David Fulton Publishers.

Tilstone, C. (1991) 'Classroom evaluation', in Tilstone, C. (ed.) *Teaching Pupils with Severe Learning Difficulties: Practical Approaches.* London: David Fulton Publishers.

Wragg, E. C. (1994) *An Introduction to Classroom Observation.* London: Routledge.

Yule, W. (1987) 'Identifying problems: functional analysis, and observation and recording techniques', in Yule, W. and Carr, J. (eds) *Behaviour Modification for the Mentally Handicapped.* London: Croom Helm.

Chapter 3

Recording Evidence

Christina Tilstone

Observation is a process which, at a basic level, is concerned with *watching,* or at a more advanced level, systematically investigating. It involves *making judgements* about what is seen, which are made either hurriedly and superficially or after a reflective analysis of carefully collected evidence. Strategies used to record evidence are as varied and as wide-ranging as the observation techniques themselves. On the one hand, comparatively loose, open-ended ways of reconstructing events and documenting information through field notes or diaries can be used; on the other, focused, preordained, elaborately constructed rating scales and observation schedules. All are useful and will yield different results. Recording evidence does not necessarily involve direct observation, and interviews, questionnaires and photographs are also effective methods of data collection. Strategies can be grouped under the following headings:

- precise designs;
- descriptions (usually after the event);
- methods other than observation.

It is not unusual for more than one strategy to be used in the search for reliable information. Using two or more strategies (sometimes referred to as 'methodologies' or 'methods' in the literature, e.g. Sanger 1996; Hopkins 1985; Fawcett 1996) to cross-examine is an important way of checking that the *evidence* collected is as accurate as possible. For example, the documentation of a pupil's work in a particular subject can be analysed alongside the continuous observations of how he approached his work, together with a video recording of his responses to specific lessons. Together they provide a detailed record which will help the teacher to develop a clear understanding of possible difficulties.

A document by SCAA (Schools Curriculum and Assessment Authority, now Qualifications and Curriculum Association (1997)) which contains information on ways of gaining a fuller understanding of children's achievements as they enter school, suggests the following sources of evidence (in addition to observations made by staff):

- dialogue between staff and children, and between the children themselves;
- conversations with parents;
- children's work (for example, writing, numerals, drawings, tape recordings, paintings, models, constructions, computer print outs).

(p.7)

Such crosschecks (referred to as 'triangulation'), using a variety of methods to obtain data, are often considered as lending credibility to the conclusions reached (Vulliamy and Webb 1992). Obviously such a *Sherlock Holmes' approach* can be beneficial but the value of the systematic use, over a period of time, of a single observational technique and the subsequent data collection should not be underestimated.

In an attempt to define different ways in which evidence can be cross-checked, Denzin (1978; 1985) lists a number of categories of triangulation, among which are:

- *theory triangulation*, when theories are tested against each other;
- *data triangulation*, in which several individuals scrutinise the data collected;
- *investigator triangulation*, which entails several individuals using the same strategies (often at different times) to crosscheck the evidence;
- *methodological triangulation*, where different strategies are used to investigate the results.

Theory triangulation usually involves the testing of existing theories in new situations, in testing existing theories against each other, or against an emerging one. Does the triangulation of the theory of grief when applied to bereavement, for example, apply to all families when first told that their son or daughter has profound multiple learning difficulties? How does Piaget's theory of assimilation and accommodation compare with the 'behaviourists' theory of learning, which involves setting conditions, antecedents and consequences?

Data triangulation involves a number of investigators analysing the same data and coming to an agreement on the conclusion. Thomas (1997), for example, in research which explored the relationship between how children held their pens or pencils and specific learning difficulties, stated that there was a 82 per cent agreement between two observers on the exact gripping positions recorded.

33

Invesigator triangulation can be used in a variety of ways and Elliott and Adelman (1976) are among the researchers who used triangulation to compare accounts of classroom events seen through the eyes of different people involved in an action. A teacher, a pupil, and the support assistant would, for example, present their own accounts of the ways in which the pupil worked with his peers during a particular activity. The example of exploring the difficulties experienced by a pupil in a specific subject (given above) involved the mixing of methods (methodological triangulation). Not only was the pupil observed and videoed, but examples of his work were also collected and analysed.

Vulliamy and Webb (1992) also refer to 'saturation' and the search for 'negative instances' as other methods of crosschecking data. Once conclusions have been reached from an analysis of the data, the investigator seeks to find examples which might disprove the theory or to scrutinise the data for alternative explanations:

> Seeking examples which disprove emerging hypotheses leads to a progressive refinement and modification of them until a point is reached when a succession of new data merely reinforces the existing categories – at which point they are said to be 'saturated'. (pp.223–4)

Recordings of data are, of course, most reliable if noted at the time of the event; a golden rule which is sometimes not practical and therefore some recordings may have to be logged as soon after the event as possible. The recording of evidence in field notes and diaries can be an effective strategy when used to collect post-event information. Whatever the strategy selected, it will naturally depend upon:

- the purpose of the investigation;
- the focus of the investigation (e.g. a single child, a group of children or an event);
- the observation techniques used;
- the time allowed;
- the time available to analyse the data;
- the circumstances under which the investigation is taking place (e.g. in the playground or in the classroom);
- the time of day;
- other adults available;
- the personal preferences of the investigator.

As with observation techniques, some recording strategies are more applicable to either quantitative or qualitative approaches, although many are applicable to both.

Strategies

Precise designs

Strategies requiring precise designs can be subdivided into observation schedules, rating and category scales, and checklists. Although it appears to be generally believed that they are highly complicated and that those who devise them need specific training, most teachers implement simple observation schedules as a matter of course (Bell, 1987). Possibly the most familiar is a basic ABC chart (Table 3.1) designed to record the triggers which precede, and the consequences of, challenging behaviours. Not only will the chart be familiar to many teachers, but the behaviours presented will be easily recognisable!

Table 3.1 ABC of Behaviour

Name of pupil: Colin W...

Date/Time	Antecedents	Behaviour	Consequences
01/11/97			
11.00	enters art room sits at table	bangs head with fist and screams	teacher moves him away from table
11.05	sits on chair in middle of room	bangs head with both fists and screams (high-pitched)	teacher encourages him to use brush to put glue onto polystyrene picture with physical prompt
11.07	works with teacher	hums quietly	absorbed in task with teacher
11.15	teacher moves away to work with another pupil	gives high-pitched scream, bangs head with fist, throws self off chair	teacher helps him back to chair

Specific observation techniques will obviously predetermine the type of schedule to be used, and the examples below are of schedules used for:

- event (Table 3.2);
- duration (Table 3.3);
- interval recording (Table 3.4).

The first two were designed for use with a pupil with profound and multiple learning difficulties; the third for a pupil with special educational needs and was used in this case with pupils with moderate learning difficulties.

Table 3.2 Event Recording Schedule (to record the frequency of specific behaviours)

Name of pupil:
Observer:
Topic: Communication of needs and wants
Date:
Behaviour: Eye pointing
Particular instructions: Please record the length of time the pupil fixes his eyes on an object, which it is thought he might want.
Context: Please provide as much detail as possible.

Object	Eye pointing	Consequence

Table 3.3 Duration Recording Schedule (to ascertain how long behaviours or actions last)

Name of pupil:
Observer:
Topic: Communication of needs and wants
Date:
Behaviour: Eye pointing
Particular instructions: Please record the length of time the pupil fixes his eyes on an object, which it is thought he might want.
Context: Please provide as much detail as possible.

Antecedent (Object)	Behaviour (Length in seconds)	Consequence (Reinforcement)

Table 3.4 Interval Recording Schedule (to record the specific behaviours of up to 7 children at 15-minute intervals) (from Ayers *et al.* 1993)

Fixed interval sampling

	Date	

| Pupil | | Class | | No. in class | | Observer | |

| Activity | | Class Behaviour Rating -2 -1 +1 +2 | Setting | |

00	15	30	45	00	15	30	45	00	15	30	45	00	15	30	45	00	15	30	45	(1) On Task	(2) Talking	(3) Looking	(4) Physical	(5) Movement	(6) Fidgeting	(7) Noise	(8) Other

More sophisticated schedules are often needed in which behaviour is categorised, but before spending time on devising such schedules it is useful to ask the following questions:

- How often will the schedule be used and by whom?
- What categories will be needed?
- Can the categories help to detect actual differences in situations?
- How can the system be as objective as possible?
- How easily can the system be analysed?

It is also necessary to pilot sophisticated systems in order to test for 'validity' (i.e. 'the extent to which an item measures or describes what it is supposed to measure or describe', Bell 1987, p.51). After testing, the schedule is, if necessary, revised. The procedure is particularly important in large scale research projects or when questionnaires and interviews are used to gather data (Blaxter *et al.* 1996).

Category systems

The most widely used category systems are those which consider the interactions between pupils and pupils, and pupils and teachers. Although Bales (1950) was one of the first to attempt to describe and categorise the behaviour of groups, the Flanders system of interactional analysis (FIAC) is the best known (Flanders 1970). The system requires observers to record the interactions taking place in the classroom every three seconds and to enter the category number on a prepared chart. Although FIAC is an extremely useful tool, teachers need a period of training and practice in its use. Hopkins (1993) points out that it does not include non-verbal communication and that some of its categories are broad and lacking in discrimination.

Flanders' ideas have been used creatively to develop other systems of analysis (Merritt and Wheldall 1986; 1978). The latter authors introduced a 'behavioural orientation' into the OPTIC (Observing Pupils and Teachers in the Classroom) observation schedule and in one section suggested the following categories of pupil activity:

O on task: looking at study materials, reading, writing, cutting, drawing;
G gross motor movement: turning round, rocking chair, waving legs;
V verbalising: calling out, talking to neighbours;
A aggression: touching, hitting, poking, pushing;
Y any other behaviour: daydreaming, gazing around; watching other children.

Probably the best known and most creative adaptation of Flanders' work for pupils with severe learning difficulties was that of Robson (undated), who in an attempt to encourage language development through structured teaching, devised schedules to record the amount of teacher language in contrast with the amount of language used by a child during a ten-minute interaction.

An example of a schedule which concentrates on the length and amount of utterances by a teacher and a pupil at the beginning of a lesson is given in Table 3.5. Robson defines utterances as 'sentences or phrases', which are usually separated by a pause. In the child's case it does not have to be grammatically correct, and an 'utterance' may be a single word, or only a sound. One of Robson's concerns was that teachers of children who had difficulty in communicating tended to talk too much and to fill 'silences' with talk, and the child, therefore, was deprived of the opportunity to develop his own language skills. The work also highlighted the need to match teacher language to the child's ability to comprehend. He suggested a number of ways of simplifying language, three of which were:

- reducing the number of words: a single word 'dog', for example, is likely to be clearer than 'there is a big dog who is waving his tail';
- reducing the complexity of the sentence structure: a short sentence is easier to understand;
- avoiding the use of negatives: a child with limited comprehension is likely to pick up the *last* thing said to him. Therefore the animal which 'is not a pig' may well *become* 'a pig' to him.

Although the work was carried out some years ago Table 3.5 provides a useful example of a simple schedule designed to record interactions.

Wragg (1994) reminds us that category systems and rating scales often appear objective but are, in practice, subjective as the criteria for judging the behaviour is not transparent. The system devised by Merrett and Wheldall (above) gives some indication of the criteria for categorising behaviours, but Wragg suggests that many teacher construct systems that fall into the trap of using ambiguous wording. He provides the following examples:

> *pupil happily reads book* (covers two types of category: 'action' and 'mood');
> *teacher shows interest* (too vague, target of interest not clear, better to qualify it);
> *pupil misbehaves and is told off* (two consecutive acts; should be coded separately).

> (p.22)

Table 3.5 Teacher language

Name of pupil

Observer:

Topic:

Date:

Number of words per utterance	Teacher	Child
1st utterance:		
2nd utterance:		
3rd utterance:		
4th utterance:		
5th utterance:		
6th utterance:		
7th utterance:		
8th utterance:		
9th utterance:		
10th utterance:		

Instructions

First: Count the number of words in both the *first ten* of the teacher's and the *first ten* of the child's utterances.

Second: Count the *number* of utterances. Enter one tick in the box below for each of the *teacher's* utterances.

Number of utterances:				

Medley (1985) emphasises that *objectivity* will depend upon the clarity of the description of the focus or category, but that it is equally important to consider the practicality of the schedule:

- how easy it is to use;
- the time taken to record the observations.

Checklists

Checklists are often used by practitioners to track the developmental progress of pupils across settings and over time. Those most frequently used are concerned with early assessment and many are available commercially. Table 3.6 gives a flavour of the assessment and developmental checklists available for use with pupils with learning difficulties (most of which are particularly useful for those at the early stages of development). It is by no means complete.

Table 3.6 Assessment and developmental checklists

General development
- *Portage checklists* (White and Cameron 1978);
- *PIP Charts* (Jeffree and McConkey 1976);
- *Stycar Sequences* (Sheridan 1977);
- *Assessment in Infancy: Ordinal Scales of Psychological Development* (Uzgiris and Hunt 1975).

Language and communication
- *Derbyshire Language Scheme* (Knowles and Masidlover 1982);
- *Living Language* (Locke 1985);
- *Assessing Communication* (Latham and Miles 1997);
- *Affective Communication Assessment* (ACA) (Coupe *et al.* 1985);
- *Learning to use a Switch* (Detheridge 1996).

Self-help and personal adequacy
- *Pathways to Independence* (Jeffree and Cheseldine 1982);
- *Assessment of Early Feeding and Drinking Skills* (Coupe *et al.* 1987).

Practitioners usually find it necessary to supplement the ticking of checklists with additional comments which will lead to deeper probes into the behaviours or the situations. One of the advantages of checklists is that they can be completed by more than one adult and can therefore provide convergent or divergent information (Boehm and Weinberg 1997). Their usefulness will depend on whether they contain all the necessary headings to produce an adequate picture of the child or the school situation. For practitioners who wish to devise their own checklists, or add items to existing ones, Boehm and Weinberg (1997) provide the following information:

- review the checklist and determine whether the items are clear and cover the content area in sufficient detail;
- practise using the checklist, with a partner if possible, in order to assess the ease with which judgements can be made and the extent to which another observer is likely to note the same behaviours;
- discuss the agreements and disagreements and make the necessary changes to the lists;
- take into account the special needs presented by individual children and the behaviours demonstrated from different cultures in order to determine whether these needs are reflected in the items;
- ensure that there is space on the checklist to comment on the context and on the appropriateness of materials (if applicable).

(adapted from Boehm and Weinberg 1997)

These authors offer a general format for teachers devising their own lists which includes the four headings (of behaviours, date, context and comments) placed horizontally across a page. Devisers of checklists for *assessment* purposes may also need to state the criteria which determine whether the item they have chosen to list can be regarded as completed or not. Criterion, the standard by which something can be judged or decided, can be a simple statement of:

- the number of *times* a behaviour needs to occur to be acceptable:
  Behaviour:　　　　Can build a tower of four bricks
  Criterion:　　　　on three separate occasions.
  (of acceptable performance)
- or the *length* of time a behaviour occurs;
  Behaviour:　　　　Can concentrate on a task
  Criterion:　　　　for five minutes.
  (of acceptable performance)
- or on the *way* a task is accomplished;
  Behaviour:　　　　Can walk down stairs
  Criterion:　　　　with one foot on a tread.
  (of acceptable performance)

Methods of devising checklists in this way have their roots in behavioural psychology, and may produce a useful formula for gaining specific information, but their limitations need to be acknowledged.

Assessment checklists devised in this manner may not have the potential for recording incidental learning or for comments on the way in which the learning has taken place.

Descriptions (often after the event)

Field notes, logs, diaries and nudge sheets are useful strategies for the recording of evidence either as reminders of the significant events during a lesson or period of time, or as running commentaries over an extended period. Field notes and logs do not usually follow a precise design, but are factual descriptions of either *continuous* or *specific* incidents and events, recorded as they happen or as soon after their occurrence as possible. In order to be objective it is important to write down only what is seen and to avoid inferential terms which cannot be verified (a point discussed in more detail in Chapter 5). As has already been stated in Chapter 1, some degree of subjectivity is unavoidable, and if the field notes are being constructed after an event, it is likely that they will reflect greater observer bias. In an effort to record as accurately as possible, it may be helpful to note down single words to trigger the memory and to supply a framework which can be filled out later. Sketches and diagrams can be helpful; *aides-mémoire* also provide supportive evidence. It is important to note the context in which the observed behaviour occurred for, as Boehm and Weinberg (1997) emphasise, particularly in relation to the logging of challenging behaviours, records of this kind may assume undue importance (see Chapter 6). The checklist in Table 3.7 proved a useful reminder of the important information required on the *context* of the enquiry in a research project which involved using post-observational field notes to record information on children with Down's syndrome in a mainstream setting (O'Hanlon and Turner 1998).

Bogdan and Bilken (1982) offer some basic, common-sense (but often neglected) ideas to simplify the process of analysis such as, numbering the pages of the field notes or logs and giving a title, a location and a date to each note. They also suggest that, when significant events or incidents are being recorded, a section should be given over to written reflections, which deals with, for example: connections between emerging patterns; themes; and points to be clarified. The uses of field notes are endless and Biott and Easen (1994) give examples of teachers using them with classes of 4- and 5-year-olds, primarily to gain general impressions of the classroom and, when analysed, to identify emerging social structures such as:

- the children's use of rules, authority and control;
- their concerns for getting it *right*, being praised and showing others to be wrong;
- their strategies for involving others.

These authors used a second set of field notes, devised from the first, to identify how the children negotiated within the social framework of the classroom and, at the same time, conformed to the expectations of their teachers.

A teacher in a special school, instead of letting the themes emerge as in the last example, used those already identified by the research of Biott and Easen (1994) as a starting point for the analysis of his field notes with a class of 15-year-old pupils with social, emotional and behavioural difficulties. The three themes became the criteria on which he made judgements about:

- the classroom organisation;
- the quality of group work;
- pupils' self-esteem;
- the levels of interaction.

By using an already established theory this *practical theoriser* then tested his own theories.

Table 3.7 Checklist for the 'context' of the observation

Observers must note:
- the date
- the time of day
- the length of the investigation (Were you present for a whole lesson or part of a lesson?)
- the activity or activities in which the class was engaged
- the activity or activities in which the child with Down's syndrome was engaged
- the layout of the classroom
  - the seating arrangements
  - the location of the teacher
- the level of individual support
- the relationship of peers to the child with Down's syndrome
- special equipment

Table 3.8 Layout of a diary

Monday 24 January 19..

Contact (person or group)	Subject (of contact)	Method (of contact)	Initiator	Rating	Reason	Other (place or time)	Comments
2nd Year S/d students	Discussion IT/In-set	F.2F	Me	1	To discuss students' concerns	FP2 09.45– 10.30	
Roy	Time-tabling problems	Tel	Me	1	Major blocks to progress	5 mins	
Val	Time-tabling problems	Tel	Me	3	No information on major blocks to progress	5 mins	
Geoff/Roy Principal	Action plan	Paper	Me	1	Development	5 mins	

Wednesday 26 January 19..

Contact (person or group)	Subject (of contact)	Method (of contact)	Initiator	Rating	Reason	Other (place or time)	Comments
Roger	IT/In-set	F2F	Me	5	Admin	Race-awareness meeting (5 mins)	
Audrey A.	Mr Howarth (DES). Rearranged visit	Memo	Audrey	3	Admin		
Geoff H.	Meeting with Principal tomorrow	Tel	Me	1	Information	Evening (15 mins)	

Keeping a diary

A diary, used in a similar way to field notes, can provide an alternative to making notes on broader issues or on particular examples of concerns or critical events, which it may be necessary to explore later in more detail. In research, field notes and diaries can involve the use of a schedule to log and to categorise specific points. Table 3.8 is an example of how a diary was used simply to record the conversations with students and staff when the writer introduced a controversial school experience scheme into a BEd programme. The importance of the contact was rated on a 1:5 scale, which over a period showed emerging patterns and trends in interest and support as the scheme developed.

Nudge sheets

Bailey (1991) advocates the use of a checklist or nudge sheet as an *aide mémoire* to allow an observer to gather evidence about the main features within a classroom. Bailey's nudge sheet takes the example of a checklist for the context of the classroom (O'Hanlon and Turner 1998) further, and asks questions under the following headings:

- the classroom as a working environment;
- physical settings;
- task-related factors;
- to what extent did the teacher...?;
- communication issues.

It was developed for use by members of staff working together in order to find out if:

- suitable conditions were established for learning to take place;
- pupils were able to access the materials in order to undertake the tasks;
- activities were suitable for the children's ages and stages of learning;
- opportunities existed for pupils to talk, to discuss and to develop language.

Although the nudge sheet involved teachers working in partnership (see Chapter 4) and was completed as each lesson progressed, it provided valuable ideas for a teacher working on her own and could be adapted to re-create important features *after* the session. In order to give a flavour of Bailey's work Table 3.9 lists the questions posed under his fourth heading.

Table 3.9 Section of a nudge sheet (from Bailey 1991)

To what extent did the teacher:

- show a firm yet friendly, relaxed and encouraging attitude to the pupil(s)?
- secure and retain the attention of the pupil(s) when necessary?
- time the lesson/activity appropriately?
- provide for progression in learning?
- cope with differences in ability level?
- use praise and other forms of encouragement?
- provide opportunities for pupils to take decisions about and responsibility for their own learning?
- move around the classroom to assist or work with individual pupils/groups of pupils?
- anticipate and avoid difficult behaviour?
- deal with minor interruptions?
- allow pupils to comment on or mark their own work?
- incorporate multicultural issues into her teaching?
- demonstrate a variety of teaching methods?
- provide clear instructions?
- use unscripted incidents/comments by children to enhance learning?
- use the curricular activities provided for the pupils to assess their progress?
- use information technology as an integral part of teaching?

Obtaining feedback from pupils

A carefully constructed nudge sheet, completed at the end of a lesson, could also provide opportunities for pupils to be involved in feedback on the topic under review. Hopkins as far back as 1985, advocated that, if possible, pupils should also keep daily logs as part of a feedback system and suggested that they are particularly useful in providing a pupil perspective on a teaching episode. Teachers of children with special educational needs are well aware, through the *Code of Practice on the Identification and Assessment of Special Educational Needs* (DfE 1994), that children should be involved in decisions on meeting their special educational needs. Fuelled by the innovations introduced as a result of the 'record of achievement' movement, such involvement stretches from initial assessment (Rose, McNamara and O'Neil 1996) to teaching as a dialogue which involves learning from children about the processes of being taught and the effect that teachers have on their work (Byers 1994;

Charlton 1996). Galloway and Davie (1996) emphasise the need for a 'listening culture' within each school, including the need for teachers and pupils to give feedback to each other by responding to their joint experiences and perceptions, as well as by expressing feelings and ideas. Wade and Moore (1993), in a survey of 115 primary and secondary teachers, found that less than a third took account of the views of pupils in any way. Interestingly, in research undertaken by McKelvey and Kyriacou (1985), the reasons for a reluctance to collect evidence through feedback from pupils was not because teachers were concerned about the quality of the information, but that the practice of obtaining information could be seen as undermining their authority. In contrast, research by Vulliamy and Webb (1991) indicated that when teachers did take account of the views of pupils in school-based action research projects their attitudes changed as they began to value their pupils' comments on all aspects of school work.

Asking pupils for feedback should be a natural model when one considers that, in adapting to school life, a pupil's *own* words and deeds are constantly being evaluated by school staff. Innovative methods have been devised to encourage pupils, including those with profound and multiple learning difficulties, to express opinions using alternative and augmentative communication, particularly through the use of symbols and computer technology (see for example, Detheridge and Detheridge 1997).

Children as researchers

Processing skills (including observing, hypothesising, questioning, recording, planning, interpreting, reflecting, and communicating) are firmly embedded in all subjects of the National Curriculum. The ORACLE project in the 1980s encouraged teachers and pupils to note similar experiences and to compare them (Galton *et al.* 1980), but highlighting these skills in a curriculum which is accessible to all children must encourage us to use the pupils' emerging research skills to the full. They should be regarded as researchers in their own right, and be encouraged to feedback their experiences in whatever way is accessible to them, which may include the use of educational technology; research diaries and note books; collections of work with commentaries; and their own nudge sheets.

Methods other than observation

Although this book is concerned with the collection of evidence through observation, it is not the only method available and it is important to consider briefly others (readily accessible to the busy practitioner) and the reasons for using them.

Video and audio recording

There are two main advantage of video and audio recording in the collection of data. Firstly, they can form part of a permanent record, and *action replays* can be used as often as required. Secondly, they provide opportunities for groups of professionals to make detailed analyses and to use a wide range of skills to interpret the evidence. Wragg (1994) makes the important point that pupils can also be involved in the interpretations, and Lomas (1995), in examining the use of video recording in assessment in a special school for pupils with visual impairments and physical disabilities, suggests that an additional advantage is the opportunity that it provides to focus on non-verbal interactions.

Cavendish *et al.* (1990), however, list the disadvantages as:

- the camera gives a selective view of the actions or behaviours under review;
- the analysis of the recording is complex and time-consuming;
- equipment is not always readily available.

The storage and indexing of tapes may also prove difficult, but a frequently underestimated problem is the reaction of some children to the presence of the equipment, despite adequate familiarisation. In a small-scale study of the methods of communication used spontaneously by children with profound and multiple learning difficulties to indicate their needs and wants, it was found that, despite careful positioning of the camera, some children were producing *atypical* responses, which could be identified as either abnormal amounts of neutral or totally passive behaviour or an exceptional number of *startled* responses. Control conditions were set up and it was concluded after some weeks that unless sophisticated equipment (including zoom lenses and purpose-built observation positions) was used, video recordings of some children in the study did not represent a true picture of their abilities (Tilstone 1989).

Audio recording, on the other hand, is less obtrusive and easier to undertake in the classroom. It has proved successful in mainstream classrooms and teachers in the Ford Teaching Project (Elliott and Adelman 1976), for example, regarded audio recording as their most important research tool. It is particularly useful in teaching children with learning difficulties, when *teacher talk* is the focus of investigation. Wragg (1994), however, mentions the loss of important visual clues and variable sound quality as being disadvantages, making it difficult to identify individual children when the acoustics are poor, and that it is often necessary to make extensive notes in order to obtain a clear understanding of the context of the recording.

Still photography

Many authors, including McCormick and James (1983), document the successful use of still photography in the collection of information, particularly when evidence is being collected to evaluate lessons.

> Although it is highly selective, depending heavily on the judgements of the cameraman, the uncertainty or ambiguity inherent in still photographs or slides appears to be a useful device to get pupils and teachers to talk about the lesson subsequently.
>
> (p.198)

Walker and Wiedel (1985) are among the researchers who have used photographs to elicit secondary pupils' responses to science lessons, and Barrett (1986) adopted a similar approach in order to obtain information on children's reactions to their first days in school.

Questionnaires

Questionnaires are a quick, and relatively simple, way of obtaining detailed information on all aspects of professional work. They need, however, to be completed and returned promptly and the results analysed as quickly as possible. The devising of questionnaires is an under-estimated skill and their advantages and disadvantages are well summed up by Hopkins (1985) in Table 3.10.

Imaginative approaches have been used to devise questionnaires as a method of pupil feedback in both mainstream and special education. Cavendish *et al.* (1990) highlight the use of cartoons to encourage children to evaluate science activities, and the National Curriculum Council (1992) gives examples of the use of visual materials which encourage children at early levels of development to provide 'yes' or 'no' responses, particularly to pictures and symbols.

Table 3.10 The advantages and disadvantages of questionnaires (adapted from Hopkins 1985)

Advantages	Disadvantages
• easy to administer	• analysis is time-consuming
• easy to follow up	• extensive preparation is needed to devise clear and relevant questions
• provide direct comparisons of groups and individuals	• questions which explore a subject in depth are difficult to construct
• provide feedback on – attitudes – the adequacy of teacher help – preparation for the next session • conclusions at the end of a term – data is quantifiable	• respondents (especially children) may try to produce the *right* answers

Interviews

Interviews and questionnaires are methods of indirect observation insofar as they may be used to provide accounts of events which can then, to some extent, be reconstructed. Both methods can provide information on motives, attitudes, values and beliefs. Lewis (1991) is one of the many writers who highlight the importance of interviews with children as a means of monitoring learning strategies. Interviews, at any level (either in work with adults or with children with or without special educational needs) can be classified as structured and unstructured and can be interpreted as points on a continuum: the predetermined, precisely worded questions of structured interviews at one end; the non-directive, with interviewees dictating their own points for discussion, at the other. McCormick and James (1983) list three other types of interview, which lie somewhere between these extremes:

- The *focused* interview, which takes a particular prespecified situation or event as the subject of the interview, then, using a set of general guidelines, tries to explore the respondent's perceptions of the situation or events.
- The *semi-structured* interview, which involves a carefully worded set of questions and predetermined responses combined with open-ended questions allowing respondents to formulate their replies, which are then carefully noted by the interviewer.

- The *informal conversational* interview, which presupposes nothing about what may be learnt. The interviewer follows the respondent's flow of ideas and makes notes after the event.

(p.204)

Lewis (1991) uses the interviews with children as a method of monitoring their perceptions of their progress as they are engaged in tasks. She adopts the term 'child-adult conference' to describe the reciprocal nature of the process in order to emphasise the importance of the sharing nature of a procedure in which a pupil and an adult exchange information on the learning involved in a specific activity. Such conferences provide rich data on the learning process and also deepen the relationship between child and adult. In a busy classroom, success will depend on the organisation necessary to facilitate the conference as much as on the teacher's ability to encourage the pupil to explain what he is doing. Lewis gives some useful pointers for setting up and implementing such conferences, three of which are:

- conferences cannot be hurried; time is needed to obtain detailed information and therefore conferences may occur infrequently;
- the other pupils will need to be discouraged from interrupting;
- tape recording is a useful means of data collection. The results can be played back to the pupil who can then be encouraged to comment on the interaction.

The questions which she suggests should be asked (the *nudge sheet*) in order to obtain a full picture of the pupil's response to the teaching, take into account:

- the prompting necessary to complete the task;
- whether the pupil can explain why he is carrying out the activity in a particular way;
- whether he is able to transfer the learning to other situations;
- his ability to respond to a variety of questions;
  for example, during a science lesson
    '...what happened when we...?'
    '...could it have been done in a better way?'
    '...what might happen if we...?'
    '...how do you feel about...?'

(pp.41–42)

Booth and Booth (1996) favour using narrative methods in order to gain access to the perspectives and experiences of people with learning difficulties. They have used a story-telling approach, over an extended period, to encapsulate the experience of growing up for someone with severe learning difficulties whose parents also had learning difficulties. The method included painstakingly piecing together a story by the elimination of alternatives, and the researchers suggest that *ruling things out* can be as revealing as a wealth of detail. They conclude that:

> ... conventional research methods can create obstacles for inarticulate subjects in terms of the demands they make on their inclusion. The lesson to be drawn from Danny's story is that researchers should attend more to their own deficiencies than to the limitations of the informers.

> (p.67)

Another form of interview, the *group interview*, is also a particularly useful method of obtaining feedback from pupils for curriculum development and planning. Schools are one of the few places where individuals spend a number of hours together in groups and it seems important, therefore, for any evaluation of the learning which takes place *alongside* others to be carried out *with* others. It is not unusual for peers to act as advocates for those who have communication problems, and a group of 16- to 19-year-olds with learning difficulties skilfully interpreted the views of three of their peers with severe physical and communication problems on the advantages and disadvantages of the school's system of Records of Achievement to an interviewer who was unknown to them (Tilstone 1991).

Interviews provide opportunities for the development of social relationships, and can thus take into account verbal and non-verbal signals. Potts (1992) suggests that an important part of the interviewing process of either individuals or groups is the 'exploration of the meanings assigned by the interviewees themselves to the events and feelings they describe' (p.335).

Summarising information

The recording of evidence can result in large amounts of data which often need to be summarised, and totals, averages and simple diagrams are quick and easy ways of providing visual representations of records to indicate general trends. For information on the analysis and presentation of extensive data, including the construction of bar and pie charts, and the use of histograms and other statistical techniques, the following are recommended:

- Bassey, M. (1995) *Creating Education through Research.* Edinburgh: Kirklington Moor Press. (British Educational Research Association.)
- Bell, J. (1997) *Doing Your Research Project, 2nd edn.* Milton Keynes: Open University Press.
- Blaxter, L., Hughes, C. and Tight, M. (1996) *How to Research.* Milton Keynes: Open University Press.
- Cohen, L. and Manion, L. (1994) *Research Methods in Education,* 4th edn. London: Routledge.

For information using computers in the analysis of results the reader is referred to:
- Fielding, N. G. (1991) *Using Computers in Qualitative Research.* London: Sage.
- Weitzman, E. (1995) *Computer Programs for Qualitative Data Analysis.* London: Sage.
- Brymzan, A. and Cramer, D. (1993) *Quantitative Data Analysis for Social Scientists.* London: Routledge.

References

Bailey, T. (1991) 'Classroom observation: a powerful tool for teachers', *Support for Learning* **6** (1), 32–6.

Bales, R. F. (1950) *Interaction Process Analysis: a Method of Studying Small Groups.* Reading, Mass: Addison-Wesley.

Barrett, G. (1986) *Starting School: an Evaluation of the Experience* (final report of an evaluation of reception children in school). Commissioned by AMMA.

Bassey, M. (1995) *Creating Education through Research.* Edinburgh: Kirklington Moor Press. (British Educational Research Association.)

Blaxter, L., Hughes, C., Tight, M. (1996) *How to Research.* Buckingham: Open University Press.

Bell, J. (1987) *Doing Your Research Project.* Milton Keynes: Open University Press.

Bell, J. (1993) *Doing Your Research Project*, 2nd edn. Buckingham: Open University Press.

Boehm, A. E. and Weinberg, R. A. (1997) *The Classroom Observer*, 3rd edn. NY: Teachers' College Press.

Bogdan, R. C. and Bilken, S. K. (1982) *Qualitative Research for Education.* London: Allyn and Bacon.

Booth, T. and Booth, W. (1996) 'Sounds of silence: narrative research with inarticulate subjects', *Disability and Society* **11** (1), 55–75.

Brymzan, A. and Cramer, D. (1993) *Quantitative Data Analysis for Social Scientists.* London: Routledge.

Byers, R. (1994) 'Teaching as a dialogue: teaching approaches and learning styles in schools for pupils with learning difficulties', in Coupe O'Kane, J. and Smith, B. (eds) *Taking Control: Enabling People with Learning Difficulties.* London: David Fulton Publishers.

Cavendish, S., Galton, M., Hargreaves, L. and Harlen, W. (1990) *Observing Activities.* London: Paul Chapman.

Charlton, T. (1996) 'Listening to pupils in classrooms and schools', in Davie, R. and Galloway, D. (eds) *Listening to Children in Education.* London: David Fulton Publishers.

Cohen, L. and Manion, L. (1994) *Research Methods in Education*, 4th edn. London: Routledge.

Coupe, J., Aherne, P., Crawford, N., Herring, J., Jolifee, J., Levy, D., Malone, J., Murphy, D., Alder, J. and Pott, P. (1987) *Assessment of Early Feeding and Drinking Skills.* Manchester: MEC.

Coupe, J., Barton, L., Barber, M., Collins, L., Levy, D. and Murphy, D. (1985) *Affective Communication Assessment.* Manchester: MEC.

Denzin, N. (1978) *The Research Act: a Theoretical Introduction to Sociological Methods.* New York: McGraw Hill.

Denzin, N. (1985) 'Triangulation', in Husen, T. and Postlethwaite, T. (eds) *International Encyclopedia of Educational Research.* Oxford: Pergamon.

Detheridge, T. (1996) *Learning to use a Switch.* Leamington Spa: Widgit Software.

Detheridge, T. and Detheridge, M. (1997) *Literacy through Symbols.* London: David Fulton Publishers.

Elliot, J. and Adelman, C. (1976) *Innovation at the Classroom Level: a Case Study of the Ford Teaching Project.* Milton Keynes: Open University Press.

Elliott, J. (1991) *Action Research for Educational Change.* Buckingham: Open University Press.

Fielding, N. G. (1991) *Using Computers in Qualitative Research.* London: Sage.

Flanders, N. A. (1970) *Analyzing Teaching Behaviour.* Reading, Mass: Addison-Wesley.

Galton, M., Simon, B. and Croll, P. (1980) *Inside the Primary Classroom.* London: Routledge.

Hopkins, D. (1985) *A Teacher's Guide to Classroom Research.* Milton Keynes: Open University Press.

Hopkins, D. (1993) *A Teacher's Guide to Classroom Research*, 2nd edn. Milton Keynes: Open University Press.

Jeffree, D. and Chesledine, S. (1982) *Pathways to Independence.* London: Hodder and Stoughton.

Jeffree, D. and McConkey, R. (1976) *PIP Developmental Charts.* London: Hodder and Stoughton.

Knowles, W. and Masidlover, M. (1982) *Derbyshire Language Scheme.* Ripley: Private Publications.

Latham, C. and Miles, A. (1997) *Assessing Communication.* London: David Fulton Publishers.

Lewis, A. (1991) *Primary Special Needs and the National Curriculum*. London: Routledge.

Locke, A. (1985) *Living Language*. Windsor: NFER-Nelson.

Lomas, J. (1995) 'The use of video as an assessment tool', *Eye Contact*. Autumn, 23–4.

McCormick, R. and James, M. (1983) *Curriculum Evaluation in Schools*. London: Croom Helm.

McKelvey, J. and Kyriacou, C. (1985) 'Research on pupils as teacher evaluators', *Educational Studies* 11, 25–31.

Medley, D. M. (1985) 'Systematic observation schedules as measuring instruments', in Weinberg, R. A. and Wood, F. H. (eds) *Observation of Pupils and Teachers in Mainstream and Special Education Settings: Alternative Strategies*. Minnesota: University of Minnesota.

Merrett, F. and Wheldall, K. (1978) 'Playing the game: a behavioural approach to classroom management in the junior school', *Educational Review* 30 (1), 41–50.

Merrett, F. and Wheldall, K. (1986) 'Observing pupils and teachers in classrooms (OPTIC): a behavioural observational schedule for use in schools', *Educational Psychology* 6, 57–68.

National Curriculum Council (1992) *Curriculum Guidance–9: The National Curriculum and Pupils with Severe Learning Difficulties*. York: NCC.

O'Hanlon, C. and Turner, B. (1998) *An Investigation into Factors Associated with the Failure of Educational Placements for Children with Down's Syndrome at both Primary and Secondary Level* (a report for the Down's Syndrome Association). London: DSA.

Potts, P. (1992) 'Approaches to interviewing', in Booth, T., Swann, W., Masterton, M. and Potts, P. (eds) *Learning for All-1: Curricula for Diversity in Education*. London: Routledge.

Robson, C. (undated) *Language Development Through Structured Teaching*. Huddersfield: The Polytechnic in association with the Hester Adrian Research Centre, Manchester.

Rose, R., McNamara, S. and O'Neil, J. (1996) 'Promoting the greater involvement of pupils with special needs in the management of their own assessment and learning processes', *British Journal of Special Education* 23 (4), 166–71.

Sanger, J. (1996) *The Compleat Observer?: A field research guide to observation*. London: Falmer Press.

SCAA (1997) *Looking at Children's Learning: Desirable Outcomes for Children's Learning on Entering Compulsory Education*. London: SCAA.

Sheridan, M. D. (1997) *From Birth to Five Years: Children's Developmental Progress* (revised and updated). London: Routledge.

Thomas, S. (1997) 'Near-point gripping in pencil hold as a possible disabling factor in children with SEN', *British Journal of Special Education* 24 (3), 129–32.

Tilstone, C. (1989) 'Methods of observing PMLD children', *PMLD Link* 4, 1–3.

Tilstone, C. (1991) 'Pupils' views', in Tilstone, C. (ed.) *Teaching Pupils with Severe Learning Difficulties: Practical Approaches*. London: David Fulton Publishers.

Uzgiris, I. and Hunt, J. McV. (1975) *Assessment in Infancy: Ordinal Scales of Psychological Development*. Urbana: University of Illinois Press.

Vulliamy, G. and Webb, R. (eds) (1991) *Teacher Research and Educational Needs*. London: David Fulton Publishers.

Wade, B. and Moore, M. (1993) *Experiencing Special Education*. Buckingham: Open University Press.

Walker, R. and Wiedel, J. (1985) 'Using photographs in a discipline of words', in Burgess, R. (ed.) *Field Methods in the Study of Education*. Basingstoke: Falmer Press.

Weitzman, E. (1995) *Computer Programs for Qualitative Data Analysis*. London: Sage.

White, M. and Cameron, S. (1987) *Portage Early Education Programme*. Windsor: NFER-Nelson.

Chapter 4

Partnership Observation

Christina Tilstone

Introduction

It has been stressed in the previous chapters that systematic observation can be carried out by professionals working alone. This is certainly true, but such innovations as team teaching; the employment of support assistants to help to meet the needs of children with disabilities and learning difficulties; special educational needs coordinators (SENCOs); subject teachers working together; and members of the multidisciplinary team cooperating, have opened up the possibilities of staff supporting each other in the classroom. In the past, teachers often worked in isolation behind closed doors and visitors to the classroom were uncommon and usually unwelcome. Research indicated that infrequent 'observers' had a marked effect on the performance of teachers (Samph 1976) and that they, and indeed pupils, 'put on a show' (divorced from reality) in an attempt to provide what it was thought the observers might be expecting. Using microphones secretly planted in the classroom at times when observers were, and were not, present Samph found that teachers provided more praise, took on board more ideas generated by their pupils and asked more questions when others were watching. In such research, it was apparent that the teachers and observers had not collaborated on the focus or nature of the observation.

The tradition of observation without collaboration has its roots in the assessment of teaching practice where an observer would sit at the back of the classroom and make judgements on novice teachers. Such an approach was challenged in the 1980s and was replaced, in many cases, by a partnership approach to supervision (Cohn 1981; Rudduck and Sigsworth 1985), in which students were encouraged to identify aspects of their teaching and their interactions with children, which then became the focus of the tutor's observation in the classroom. Mentoring, with its model of 'on the job training', now encapsulates both partnership and collaboration.

Partnership observation involves two people working collaboratively in order to analyse, and to learn from, the events in a classroom or school. Partners can either be *outside partners* (who do not work in the school but have been invited in or who visit the school infrequently) and *inside partners* (staff from within the institution). In both cases, the object of the partnership is to offer 'another pair of friendly eyes' in order to improve the teaching and learning taking place.

Outside partners

Independent observation is used by HMI and Local Inspectors as a basis for formal and informal institutional evaluation. OFSTED style external inspections require extensive classroom observation and, unlike the early days of some teaching practice supervision, they are based on an explicit framework. *The Handbook for Inspection of Schools* (OFSTED 1993) gives criteria in addition to outlining the inspection procedures. It states that there is a need for:

- honesty, clarity, consistency and objectivity in the framing and communication of judgements;
- concern for accuracy and a respect for evidence;
- sensitivity to the circumstances of the school and of all individuals or groups connected with it;
- respect for the integrity of teachers, pupils, parents and governors;
- recognition that the interests and welfare of pupils are the first priority in relation to anything inspectors observe or about which they are informed;
- sensitivity to the impact of judgements.

Do the inspection processes in general and the classroom observations in particular have a direct impact on the development of teaching and learning within the school? What lessons can be learned from such 'outside' observations? Do the results of the observations in the classroom become the agenda for change within school?

Despite OFSTED's attempt to monitor its own processes it is, as Earley (1996) points out, difficult to disentangle the effects of inspection from the other major changes (some brought about by other legislation) that schools have undergone in the last few years. Research by OFSTED itself

(1994; 1995) claims that the inspection process is making a contribution to school improvement, but Matthews and Smith (1995) emphasise that it is the subsequent action planning (resulting in part from observation in classrooms) which leads to the greatest improvements. Other researchers (Joyce 1991; Beresford 1995; Ainscow *et al.* 1995; Hopkins *et al.* 1997) suggest that deeper cultures and organisational conditions are the key to school improvements. They include: classroom-based staff development; enquiry and reflection; and collaborative planning. Interestingly, such *deeper* conditions often hinge on 'partnerships' as mechanisms for improvement. Such considerations are discussed by Moore in Chapter 7 in relation to the role of observation in teacher appraisal.

The ingredients of any partnership in any situation: business and commerce; social work; health and education are respect, trust, commitment, common understanding and the identification of individual needs, all of which will be discussed in more detail later in this chapter. Partners, in any context, work together on what they feel is important, share their experiences, learn from each other, and provide mutual support within an analytical framework leading to accountability (Tilstone 1998).

Persuasive arguments have been developed in order to encourage teachers to invite known, respected and trustworthy outsiders to observe educational practice and to provide an objective view (May and Sigsworth 1982; Rudduck 1987; Visser 1987). In the 1980s, May and Sigsworth reported that it was usual for outside observers to be colleagues from institutions of higher education or university lecturers having an already established professional relationship with a teacher or a school. Now, it is equally likely that general or subject advisers from LEAs or staff from other schools within the same LEA (or even, but far less frequently, other professionals) are invited to observe some aspects of classroom practice or children's learning. Such partnerships will only work if the outsider is not regarded as an authoritarian assessor figure ('the old style teaching practice supervisor') and is able to take on the role of facilitator, with the teacher in control of the direction of the observation and the consequent actions. The job descriptions of some teacher advisers (where they still exist in the present economic climate) may include this role. A useful alternative might be to establish a consortium of teachers from neighbouring schools within which such partnerships can develop. If the status of observation is raised to a level where an observation culture develops within schools, staff will find innovative ways of watching each other work in order to improve teaching and learning.

Lewisham is one LEA which has recognised the power of outside observers. In planning its new education service, in collaboration with the senior managers of schools, based on Local Management of Schools (LMS), the need to develop partners who would assist the self-review and the management and professional development of individual schools, was recognised (Stoll and Thomson 1997). Lewisham's inspectors and advisory teachers became members of a Quality Assurance and Development Service (QAD) which provides a critical friendship facility. Quoted in Stoll and Thomson, Costa and Kallick (1993) regard 'a critical friend' as: '... a trusted person who asks provocative questions, provides data to be examined through another lens, and offers a critique of a person's work as a friend' (p.27).

Critical friends from other disciplines and backgrounds, who are able to offer distinctive expertise as a result of differences in experience, insights and (possibly) age, may well provide additional strengths in observer partnerships. In the Lewisham experiment, such differences provided the basis for a more open exchange of ideas and views than those normally possible between staff who have worked together over a number of years. The pooling of different perspectives made such collaborations invaluable; a point often stressed in other observation partnerships (Fawcett 1996; Boehm and Weinberg 1997).

Inside partners

Tamsett (1982) suggests that teachers in mainstream schools tend to seek partners who share the same subject interests or who have the experience of teaching similar (usually problematic) groups of pupils, but he also suggests that:

> ... the qualities bound up in friendship seem to be the strongest link between the people who choose to work together, the respect of professionalism is also desirable, as well as the recognition that the partner has a serious interest in the task of teaching.
>
> (p.59)

It is interesting to note that in this and other, more recent, research on the essential ingredients of partnerships (Sanger 1996; Pollard and Tann 1993) *respect* is considered to be more important than *status*. It is unlikely that teachers concerned with children with special educational needs will be working in isolation and the idea that teaching quality is dependent on the personality or status of an individual teacher is totally unacceptable when diverse needs have to be met. The blurring of professional boundaries in order to encourage closer working relationships and the emerging emphasis on pedagogic theory (Galton 1996) and their consequent organisational demands have, I believe, led to more trusting and open relationships.

Aids to partnership

Nevertheless, all collaborative ventures need *time* to develop. Outside observers need time to make initial contacts and children need time to acclimatise to new faces in the classroom. Inside observers need time to alter the focus of their working relationships in order to take on the *shared* responsibility of improving school practice. It is also necessary for time to be set aside (away from the classroom) for the discussion of what has been observed, and for the partners to plan future actions.

Time is one of the factors which will contribute to the success of partnerships in observation. The other four, referred to at the beginning of the chapter (adapted from Lewis 1991), are:

- commitment;
- common understanding;
- the identification of individual needs;
- trust.

Commitment

Before embarking on any form of partnership observation, it is obvious that the teacher must be convinced of the advantages of the approach. Having another person observing work in the classroom can be threatening, especially when it is recognised that teaching is so complex that it is impossible to *get it right*. An outsider is often easier to accept, as it is likely that he or she lacks the intimate knowledge of the classroom and is more likely to celebrate teaching as an achievement. On the other hand, the insider has a holistic view of the classroom, but if Jackson's (1968) theory still applies, i.e. that the major function of all teachers (the observer and the observed) is as 'activity managers', it may be difficult for the person who is providing 'the second pair of eyes' to move away from limited perceptions. McCormick and James (1983) are in no doubt that '... given their inside status, it is questionable whether teachers can ever detach themselves from what has become familiar, in order to subject it to critical scrutiny.' (p.132)

But this is not a view held by the editor of this book. The definition of observation given in Chapter 1 recognises its limitations, and the statement that observation is '...the systematic, and as accurate as possible, collection of usually visual evidence leading to informed judgements and to necessary changes in accepted practices' acknowledges that some degree of subjectivity is unavoidable by any observer. 'Insiders' who work within the school have an intimate knowledge of the children, the supporting structures, and its ethos and philosophy. Consequently, the full and unique awareness of all aspects of the life of the school, that the inside observer brings to the task, can help the teacher to locate, and to act on, the observations within a set of shared experiences.

If the partners (inside and outside) are willing to accept responsibility for improving the quality of the children's learning, in terms of either product or process, they need to agree on how the gathering of evidence will be carried out. In the case of two adults from similar disciplines working together in a classroom (for example, teacher and teacher or teacher and nursery nurse) it may be advantageous in certain circumstances for the roles of observer and teacher to be interchanged, but this is a decision for the partners themselves. It is, however, possible to choose to be a *participant observer* by interacting with pupils as the need arises, rather than adopting the *fly on the wall approach* of the non-participant observer; a point returned to later in this chapter.

The elements of partnership observation

As has already been stated, time is an important element, not just in relationship-building (suggested earlier), but in carrying out work together. The pair need the time and the commitment to:

- plan the work (pre-observational stage);
- discuss the findings away from the classroom, and evaluate the effectiveness of the approach (post-observational stage);
- reflect on what has been learned;
- use the reflection to plan the next stage of the work.

(adapted from Ashton et al. undated)

Pre-observational stage

During the pre-observational discussion, partners will need to agree the principles of the procedures, clarify the focus of the observations, and decide on the practicalities, including:

63

- the kind of data needed;
- the observational techniques to be used;
- ways in which the data will be processed;
- the time available for
  - planning the work,
  - the observations themselves,
  - the follow-up discussion;
- the positioning of the observer;
- decisions on what the children will be told.

This and previous chapters have provided information on the first four practicalities. The positioning of the observer and the decisions on what to tell the children are often overlooked. If, for example, the focus of the observation is on how a child goes about a particular task, the observer will need to have a clear view of all that takes place and to be positioned as close to the 'action' as possible. If, however, the focus of the observation (as in the case of Susan in Chapter 2) is on how the child interacts with the environment and with other children and how he goes about a number of tasks, it will be necessary to view the action from different positions. Consequently, careful thought and the strategic positioning of pens, paper and chairs will be necessary in order to reduce frustration and eliminate the loss of valuable time. Wragg (1994) goes further and suggests that it is important for observers to dress in ways which do not draw attention to themselves, and that the effects of intrusion are minimised by ensuring that what is seen appears 'as natural and unstaged as possible'.

In most situations, it is desirable to tell the children the reasons for the observer's presence in the classroom. After the initial expected curiosity, most pupils quickly accept the presence of an observer as a normal occurrence and pay little attention to the 'second pair of eyes'. Clark and Leat (Chapter 5) favour involving the children as much as possible and sometimes include a debriefing session after the observation in which the child also provides information on what has been observed. The use of such *child-adult conferences* is also considered in Chapter 3. As a general rule, it is important to give children a matter-of-fact explanation of what you are doing and why.

There are, however, other important issues to consider, the first two of which are discussed in more detail in the Conclusion. The first relates to the rights of the child and his right to be consulted in all aspects of learning. The second involves ethical decisions. Observation can be construed as 'spying' and consequently the honesty and sensitivity of those involved are of the utmost importance. The third concerns the cultivation and development of the pupils' own research skills (discussed in Chapter 3), and the use of feedback. If a 'listening culture', advocated by Galloway and Davie (1996), is an essential element in the development of the effectiveness of professionals, as much information as possible on what is happening, and why, should be available to pupils.

Haydon (1986) also suggests that it is useful to consider factors which could influence observation and her list includes: the weather and the time of day; the conditions in the room (strong sunlight or a low temperature, for example); and the nature of the previous lesson. A PE lesson or a period of intensive work before the observation may affect the information gathered. Children may be tired and irritable towards the end of the school day and a sudden snowstorm or an unexpected gust of wind may provide interesting diversions which influence the learning process. A jointly compiled 'nudge sheet' devised for commenting on the context of the observation (see Chapter 3) should indicate any unusual conditions.

Post-observational stage

Making time to consider the evidence collected can be difficult, and it may not be possible for the pair (observer and observed) to hold discussions immediately after the observation. Formal arrangements need to be made if outside observers are invited into the school and time needs to be *booked* for the observation process to include not only the time to observe, but the time for discussion. Changes to the timetable and the support of the senior management team may be necessary to facilitate meetings. Organisational and structural changes are more likely if observation is given its rightful status in the school development plan as a catalyst for school improvement and as an agent of change. Its elements of enquiry (reflection; professional development; the practical involvement of staff and pupils; a commitment to collaborative planning) are all identified in the research on school development and improvement (Ainscow *et al.* 1995; Hopkins 1994; Hopkins *et al.* 1997).

Common understandings

One of the most important strategies for establishing a productive observational relationship is an agreement on the focus of the investigation. The teacher must determine, and have ownership of, the focus by nominating a topic or problem on which she would like feedback. Clarification of the task can only be achieved through open discussion in order to develop procedures and to establish a framework for action. Inevitably there will be several possible ways of exploration, but the teacher's background and experience, and teaching style and classroom management strategies may provide pointers for workable plans. Webb (1990) and Sanger (1996) stress the importance of teachers *owning* the process and they highlight the need to view and to analyse the data.

The observer, in addition to providing evidence (as impartial as possible) is in a good position to ask the kind of supportive questions which allow teachers to examine critically the values and structures which determine practice. Lindsay and Thompson (1997) emphasise the tension between value systems operating in the education of children with special educational needs. The dilemmas of equal opportunities, the constant demands for resources, the requirements of legislation, can all lead to conflicts, but perhaps the greatest dilemmas are caused by contradictory personal values. Knowledge of our own values, where and how they have been formed and how they relate to the values of others within the school are crucially important factors in meeting the needs of any child. By discussing the evidence available, the pair will be in a good position to articulate, examine and challenge their own belief systems and, consequently, to test them in practice and against each other (Bell and Dennis 1994).

Some proponents of partnership-observation (Rudduck 1982; May and Sigsworth 1982) suggest that a contract between the teacher and the observer is a useful way of defining roles, responsibilities and procedures. 'Contracts' are usually connected with formal, large-scale research projects or are set up between supervisors and students studying for higher research degrees (Phillips and Pugh 1994), but Lacey and Lomas (1993) see contracts as one of the most important mechanisms for encouraging collaboration in a range of settings, and suggest that their use is undervalued in work with children with special educational needs. Contracts may be considered to be too formal in situations where observers know each other well, but the formulation of a set of 'ground-rules' or 'agreements' can be essential precursors to action. Such rules will depend on individual situations, but the need to observe strict confidentiality is a priority.

The identification of individual needs

Personal and professional needs vary and most of us require a sense of security, self-recognition, friendliness, and the opportunity to take on responsibilities within our own capabilities. Partnership observation, whether carried out by insiders or outsiders, threatens what Rowlands

(1988) calls 'my body of knowledge', by which he means the established, highly valued teaching strategies and routines which make up a teacher's personal belief system and her survival skills. Through the process of partnership observation, two bodies of knowledge, those of the teacher and the observer, are immediately linked, and a new, shared *knowledge base* is established. The results are probably exciting and stimulating, and the situation may never be the same again but, in the process, the *knock-on effect* may expose the teacher to information, not only about what she does, but about her value judgements on pupils' learning.

An observer who is warm, caring, open and honest, and can communicate effectively will be the least threatening. Although very little has been written about the importance of communication between partners in observation, the literature on strategies for effective communication (for example, Mulligan 1988; Lacey and Lomax 1993; Easen 1985) is extensive. And, as Easen reminds us, the transactional skills of receiving information; listening; interpreting and responding; care in questioning; and the ability to summarise accurately are important and '...real communication is candid, honest, and is concerned with genuine understanding and the sharing of feelings and experiences' (p.111). He goes on to stress that communication is not easy, but well worth the effort when, in the case of partnership observation, communication supports those inevitable 'personal journeys of change'.

Trust

The last important factor in aiding partnerships in observation is trust, which is not easy to describe, but dictionary definitions include:

- a firm belief in the reliability of truth;
- confident expectations;
- honesty.

Each of these qualities is essential in the establishment of trust between observational partners. Add 'the desire to share ideas'; 'to respect the ideas of others'; and 'complete dependability', and the recipe for an *honest broker* is complete. Like all recipes, however, much depends on careful mixing!

Participant observation

Finally, participant observation needs to be considered. The discussions on partnership observations so far have centred on the observer adopting a *fly on the wall* approach, but it should be possible to observe *and* to become involved in the 'action', usually for short periods of time. Participant observation can involve observers working in partnership, as well as teachers observing within their own classrooms. Peake (1992), working with a colleague, emphasised that as the classroom enquiry progressed:

> I became increasingly involved in the activities of the individuals ... I had not anticipated the depth of my own involvement ...

> ... it was impossible for me even in my attempts at non-participatory observation, to distance myself from the group of pupils I was studying.

> (p.88)

The degree of *participation* in classroom or school activities in partnership observation will obviously depend on the nature of the focus and the decisions of the partners. At one end of the continuum, it may only amount to answering the usual questions that pupils ask when someone who is familiar to them is in, what they consider to be, 'the wrong place'. At the other end, circumstances may make it necessary for the observer to intervene by helping a child with a particular problem or by providing another pair of *hands* as well as *eyes* to deal with an unexpected occurrence (a *grand mal*, for example). In Peake's case (referred to earlier), there may be a deep-seated need on the part of the observer to become involved. In one particularly fruitful partnership observation between me, as an outside observer, and a mainstream teacher it was agreed that I would move in and out of the action as necessary. In the main, I was a non-participant observer but, when I felt that more information could be obtained from my becoming involved, I stepped in to ask a question or to provide an additional resource. The reasons for my interactions were discussed in the follow-up sessions outside the classroom. Thus my professional judgements were tested in the light of the best interests of the teaching and learning taking place through my attempt to answer the simple question, 'Why?'

As has already been stressed, observation, whether participatory or non-participatory, is never totally objective. The use of the identified techniques and strategies, together with the methods of recording (discussed in other chapters) will aid intellectual and emotional detachment, and regular practice will enhance observation skills and sharpen all aspects of the process. As has already been stressed, the *focus* can vary from concern over a particular pupil to a curriculum or organisational issue within the classroom or school. Assumptions will be constantly challenged and a number of questions will be raised for further enquiry. Systematic observation, either carried out alone or in partnership, gives teachers the means to be their own 'knowledge generators' in contrast to 'appliers' of someone else's knowledge (Gurney 1989).

References

Ainscow, M. (1993) ' Beyond special education: some ways forward', in Visser, J. and Upton, G. (eds) *Special Education in Britain after Warnock*. London: David Fulton Publishers.

Ainscow, M., Hargreaves, D. H., Hopkins, D. (1995) 'Mapping the process of change in schools', *Evaluation and Research in Education* **9** (2), 75–90.

Ashton, P. M. E., Peacock, A., Preston, M. (undated) *Doing IT-INSET: No.1. Getting Started*. Leicester: The University of Leicester (Centre for Evaluation in Teacher Education).

Bell, G. H. and Dennis, S. (1994) 'School development, networking and managing for change', in Bell, G. H. (ed.) with Stakes, R. and Taylor, G. *Action Research: Special Needs and School Development*. London: David Fulton Publishers.

Beresford, J. (1995) 'The classroom conditions scale', Cambridge: University of Cambridge, School of Education (Mimeo).

Cohn, M. (1981) 'A new supervision model for linking theory to practice', *Journal of Teacher Education* **32** (3), 26–30.

Department for Education and Employment (1995) *Inspection Quality 1994/5*. London: DfEE.

Earley, P. (1996) 'School improvements and OFSTED inspections: the research evidence', in Earley, P., Fiddler, B., Ouston, J. (eds) *Improvement Through Inspection*. London: David Fulton Publishers.

Galloway, D. and Davie, R. (eds) (1996) *Listening to Children in Education*. London: David Fulton Publishers.

Galton, M. (1996) 'Primary culture and classroom teaching: the learning relationship in context', in Kitson, N. and Merry, R. (eds) *Teaching in the Primary School*. London: Routledge.

Gurney, M. (1989) 'Implementor or innovator? a teacher's challenge to the restrictive paradigm of traditional research', in Lomax, P. (ed.) *The Management of Change: Increasing School Effectiveness and Facilitating Staff Development through Action Research*. Clevedon: Multilingual Matters.

Haydon, F. (1986) *Observation*. Leicester: The University of Leicester (Centre for Evaluation in Teacher Education).

Hopkins, D., West, M., Ainscow, M., Harris, A. and Beresford, J. (1997) *Creating the Conditions for Classroom Improvement*. London: David Fulton Publishers.

Joyce, B. (1991) 'The doors to school improvement', *Educational Leadership* **48** (8), 59–62.

Lindsay, G. and Thompson, G. (1997) *Values into Practice in Special Education*. London: David Fulton Publishers.

McCormick, R. and James, M. (1983) *Curriculum Evaluation in Schools.* London: Croom Helm.

Matthews, P. and Smith, G. (1995) 'OFSTED: inspecting schools and improvement through inspection', *Cambridge Journal of Education* **25** (1), 23–34.

May, N. and Sigsworth, A. (1982) 'Teacher-outsider partnership in the observation of classrooms', in Rudduck, J. (ed.) *Teachers in Partnership: Four Studies of In-service Collaboration* (Schools Council Programme 2). London: Longman.

Mulligan, J. (1988) *The Personal Management Handbook: How to Make the Most of your Potential.* London: Sphere Books.

OFSTED (Office for Standards in Education) (1993) *Handbook for the Inspection of Schools.* London: HMSO.

OFSTED (Office for Standards in Education) (1994) *Improving Schools.* London: HMSO.

Peake, L (1992) 'Devising motor programmes for children with physical disabilities', in Vulliamy, G, and Webb, R. (eds) *Teacher Research and Special Educational Needs.* London: David Fulton Publishers.

Phillips, E. M. and Pugh, D. S. (1994) *How To Get A PhD* (a handbook for students and their supervisors) 2nd edn. Buckingham: Open University Press.

Pollard, A. and Tann, S. (1993) *Reflective Teaching in the Primary School* 2nd edn. London: Cassell.

Rowlands, S. (1988) 'My body of knowledge', in Nias, J. and Groundwater-Smith, S. (eds) *The Enquiring Teacher: Supporting and Sustaining Teacher Research.* London: Falmer Press.

Rudduck, J. and Sigsworth, A. (1985) 'Partnership supervision (or Goldhammer Re-visited)', in Hopkins, D. and Reid, K. (eds) *Re-thinking Teacher Education.* London: Croom Helm.

Rudduck, J. (1987) 'Partnership supervision as a basis for the professional development of new and experienced teachers', in Wideen, M. F. and Andrews, I. (eds) *Staff Development for School Improvement: a Focus on the Teacher.* London: Falmer Press.

Samph, T. (1976) 'Observer effects on teacher verbal behaviour', *Journal of Educational Psychology* **68** (6), 736–41.

Stoll, L. and Thomson, M. (1997) 'Moving together: a partnership approach to improvement', in Earley, P., Fiddler, B., Ouston, J. (eds) *Improvement Through Inspection.* London: David Fulton Publishers.

Tamsett, R. (1982) 'Teacher-teacher partnerships in the observation of classrooms', in Rudduck, J. (ed.) *Teachers in Partnership: Four Studies of In-service Collaboration* (Schools Council Programme 2). London: Longman.

Tilstone, C. (1998) 'The education of children with severe learning difficulties: responding to challenge and change in the curriculum, in teaching and learning, and in teacher development'. Unpublished PhD Thesis. Birmingham: The University of Birmingham.

Visser, J. (1987) 'Teacher training and special educational needs', in Hinson, M. (ed.) *Teachers and Special Educational Needs.* London: David Fulton Publishers.

PART TWO

Chapter 5

The Use of Unstructured Observation in Teacher Assessment

Catherine Clark and Sally Leat

Introduction

Although the importance of assessing academic progress in schools, as an essential part of 'raising standards', was emphasised in the *Education Reform Act* (DES 1988) and is high on the present Government's agenda as the millennium approaches, the case for the statutory assessment of pupils 'having special educational needs' was made much earlier in the *Education Act 1981* (DES 1981). Nevertheless, in the late 1980s Goacher *et al.* (1988) found that schools still perceived assessment procedures as time-consuming and difficult to implement.

Although definitions of the appropriate criteria for the assessment of pupils with learning difficulties have proved problematical, the five stage model suggested in *The Code of Practice on the Identification and Assessment of Special Educational Needs* (DfE 1994) has made the principles of assessment clearer. But, as Fish and Evans (1995) stress, it gives teachers little guidance on ways of putting these principles into practice (Stakes and Hornby 1997).

Stage One assessments are undertaken by class and subject teachers who are expected to make the appropriate provision for any pupils with learning difficulties within the classroom. Therefore the question of how needs are assessed by teachers becomes vital. It is the responsibility of class and subject teachers, if they are concerned about any child who is not making satisfactory progress, to draw up a plan of action, with manageable learning targets to be achieved by the child within a specified timescale. If a child fails to progress satisfactorily, following review, he may then be considered for assessment at Stage Two as described in the Code of Practice 'Guidelines' (DfE 1994).

At this Stage, the Special Needs Coordinator (SENCO) often draws up and monitors an individual education plan (IEP) for the child, and becomes involved in making the appropriate provision. Again, learning targets within time limits are set and, if the child has made good progress following review, he may either be allowed to revert to Stage One assessment procedures and provision or stay at Stage Two to work on newly identified targets.

Alternatively, it may be decided that, if the child is considered to be making unsatisfactory progress at Stage Two, he should be assessed at Stage Three. At this point, the school can request help from the Local Education Authority (LEA) for the additional resources deemed necessary to ensure that the child will make progress. The assessment procedures can, theoretically, continue to Stage Four when the Local Education Authority carries out a statutory assessment of the child. At this point, detailed information is required from the parents, the school and any relevant outside agencies, such as the school medical services or the local social services department (Fogell and Long 1997), as a prerequisite for a Statement of Special Educational Needs. Whether or not the result is a Statement will ultimately depend on the judgement of the local education authority.

Although the Code of Practice (DfE 1994) has clarified the procedures for writing individual education plans, assessment remains largely a subjective activity as there are no set criteria for assessing special needs and one of the main, almost insuperable problems, is to decide *whose* needs are special and what *special* actually *means*. As 'special needs' is a relative term, the assessment of children with special educational needs will be dependent on the judgements of individual teachers. For instance, it is possible for a child to be assessed as having special educational needs at Stage One in one school but, if he changes schools, the assessment may not be accepted by the second school as accurate. Identification and assessment are likely to depend on the level of achievement in a specific school. The baseline for assessment is the standard set by each school within the framework of the National Curriculum assessment procedures. An additional factor is that, as learning support staff usually provide the additional help needed to enable children with special educational needs to access the curriculum in mainstream schools, in those local education authorities where the provision of learning support is inadequate, schools may be reluctant to place too many children at Stage Two of the Code because they are unlikely to be able to meet the extra identified needs without help from the LEA. Such a situation has serious implications for access to scarce resources, especially with the recent emphasis on 'outcome-related funding'.

It is problematical that assessment is often associated with notions of accountability and cost effectiveness, both of which are key issues as schools compete in the education 'market-place'. Fish and Evans (1995) point out that, as a result of schools being preoccupied with the implementation of the National Curriculum and its attendant examination system, little attention has been given to identifying how outcome-related funding is affecting special needs policy, practice and provision. They suggest that the 'harder to teach' pupils (for example, those with learning and behavioural difficulties) may be less attractive to schools which are able to determine their own admission policies. It would appear that the increase in the number of exclusions is a specific indicator of this trend (Cohen *et al.* 1994; Lloyd-Smith and Dwyfor Davies 1995).

If the 'harder to teach' have become less *attractive* to schools, the outlook for pupils whose needs are even more complex (including those whose learning difficulties and/or behaviour problems are severe) is problematical, despite the rhetoric of the Green Paper (DfEE 1997). For them, the expected outcomes of academic progress (considered to be appropriate for the population at large) are far less applicable. Nevertheless, changes in the allocation of funds by central Government and local education authorities are currently being considered if pupils do not demonstrate *observable* learning. It is possible that teachers and schools may then have to provide evidence of the effective and efficient use of resources, and of adequate planning, provision and practice in order to demonstrate that pupils have made measurable progress (Fletcher-Campbell 1996).

One of the fundamental reasons for developing more accurate assessment systems is, therefore, to ensure that the monitoring process is sufficiently sensitive and sophisticated for the progress, however small, of any pupil to be credited (Fletcher-Campbell and Lee 1995). The main focus of this chapter, therefore, is on a dynamic model of assessment, which teachers in busy classrooms will find manageable. Such a model combines assessment, evaluation and planning and should do justice to the efforts and outcomes of work of both pupils with learning difficulties and their teachers.

Dynamic assessment

The main aim of dynamic assessment is the continual assessment of a wide range of learning responses which are monitored thoroughly and systematically over time. Some may be predicted or expected; others may not. The model should also be capable of analysing the social, emotional and physical as well as the cognitive aspects of learning. It is essential for any assessment system for pupils with learning difficulties to measure more than the purely observable academic outcomes as suggested by SCAA (now QCA) (1996) for National Curriculum assessment. Routine assessment procedures will, of course, collect appropriate evidence of academic outcomes through the use of tests and profiles but, for pupils with learning difficulties, they will also need to take into account, as far as possible, all aspects of learning and to provide evidence of social, emotional, physical or psychological progress. In many ways, the process of routine assessment requires a reconceptualisation of learning but equally, as Ware and Healey (1994) remind us, it necessitates a 'reconceptualisation of progress'. They stress that it is essential to look at progress from the perspective of the pupil, and suggest that observational assessments may be one way forward.

The use of observation

Observation is not a new way of assessing the development of pupils. Goldbart (1994), for example, referring to the assessment of communication skills of pupils with profound and multiple learning difficulties, points out that Uzgiris and Hunt (1975), Coupe *et al.* (1985) and Goldbart together with Rigby (cited in Ware 1994) all provide the means by which even pre-intentional communication (communication at the earliest level) can be monitored. Similar schedules (some detailed; some specifically focused) are available in many other areas of child development to code observations and to make analysis straightforward. Nevertheless, the time management problems that many teachers seem to experience in busy classrooms suggest that the time taken to complete schedules may militate against their regular use. Also, structured observation schedules, owing to their underlying requirement for focus, cannot be holistic. They tend to highlight the specific and consequently are less comprehensive: they are exclusive rather than inclusive. Exclusivity is a serious limitation when observing pupils with learning difficulties, particularly those with severe learning or emotional and behavioural difficulties who may be unconventional learners involved in unconventional learning with, possibly, unconventional outcomes.

With this in mind, a small-scale study, to consider the use of different observation techniques as aids to assessment and curriculum planning, was undertaken in a primary school, in which it was common practice to refer children for extra help on the basis of an individual teacher's judgements rather than on any explicit criteria. The majority of the children referred for additional help also exhibited disruptive behaviour and, consequently, it seemed appropriate to use 'partnership observation' to observe at first-hand the classroom behaviours of these pupils. Partnership observation enables a disruptive group to be studied at the same time as a group of peers of similar ability in order to identify the extent to which disruptive behaviour influences the decisions made by teachers about their pupils' needs.

The techniques of observation

Having decided to use observation to investigate the classroom behaviours of these two groups of children (detailed below), a decision had to be made about the type of observation to be used. Observation techniques fall into two broad categories. Structured or systematic observation was developed by psychologists in the early 1920s in the United States who used observational systems of classroom behaviours to collect data for tabulation and later analysis (Delamont and Hamilton 1983). Structured observation is often used with large 'populations' in order to generate data which can be used for statistical analysis; examples of systematic observation schedules are cited in Galton's *British Mirrors* (1978) and in the well-known *Interaction Analysis Categories* (Flanders 1964). Despite its undoubted value, structured observation, owing to its underlying need for a particular focus, cannot be holistic and therefore tends to highlight the specific and is, in principle, less comprehensive. For pupils with learning difficulties it is important (as stated previously) that the observation techniques used should be sufficiently flexible to take the unexpected and the surprising into account. To date, many of the common assessment procedures have been rigid and over-focused and have not been sensitive enough to capture the subtle and the sudden as well as the obvious and the gradual.

The second category is that of unstructured or ethnographic observation, which has no predetermined categories but records as much of what happens as is possible. It is then left to the analyst to focus upon areas of particular interest. A number of considerations led to the choice of unstructured observation for this study. As it is always difficult to predict the learning and behavioural outcomes, the predetermined categories of systematic observation schedules were considered to be insufficiently flexible to capture the wide range of behaviours exhibited in classrooms. In particular, in the case of event recording, the links between the behaviour and the context in which it was observed and its antecedents and its consequences are not often recorded. For example, a child observed hitting other children may only be doing so during certain lessons, at particular times of the day, or after provocation. Simply recording a behaviour without the context in which that behaviour occurs means that a full picture is not obtained. In addition, as the study was small-scale it did not lend itself readily to the kind of quantitative analysis to which systematic observations are subjected.

Consequently, an ethnographic approach appeared to offer the best means of including more rather than fewer, behaviours and of providing links between observed behaviours and the context. By beginning with the whole and then focusing on particular areas of interest identified through an analysis of the data using Strauss's work on 'grounded theory' (1967), it was possible to generate theories on the basis of comparisons between, and among, children. This type of observation, therefore, enabled the unexpected, as well as the routine, to be included and recorded in the context of lesson type, the time of day, classroom organisation, and pupil/teacher or pupil/pupil interactions. Authors such as Delamont and Hamilton (1983) argue that even with small sample observations, important insights can be obtained, relationships between pupils and teachers clarified, common phenomena identified and generalisations attempted. Such conclusions are encouraging to small-scale researchers.

Unstructured observation is based on *what is said* (where appropriate) and *what is done*, rather than what is inferred by the observer. It is, therefore, a script of *what happened* and a way of collecting evidence relating to holistic achievement which can be used (if appropriate) with evidence from other types of (usually) summative assessment (such as tests and checklists) and normative assessments (profiles of achievement) to produce a comprehensive record of the achievements of a pupil. Drummond (1993) reminds us, however, that any '...assessment is essentially provisional, partial, tentative, exploratory, and inevitably incomplete...' (p.14), even if it sets out to be all-embracing. The transitory nature of assessment is one reason why it has to be an ongoing process as it is only over time that the evidence of learning can be observed and recorded.

A second crucial issue is the interpretation of data, especially from unstructured and, consequently, uncoded observations. The process can be complex, as the data, unlike coded data, are easily affected by the idiosyncratic views, values and beliefs of the observer. 'What we already know', 'what we are familiar with', 'what we would like to see', all influence how we respond to data about pupils and the learning process; a point already discussed in earlier chapters. No observer can be completely impartial and it is, therefore, important to acknowledge that completely impartial observations are impossible whatever schedule is used or in whatever way the data are encoded and analysed. It is in fact possible, however, during the analysis of data, to identify common phenomena, to make generalisations with regard to each child and to gain valuable insights into his classroom activities.

Easen (1985) suggests some interesting ways of undertaking data analysis from unstructured observations. He stresses that, in order to analyse the data, the teacher/researcher should devise a series of questions arising from the principal reason for undertaking the observation, which can be summarised as follows:

- *What* did the learner learn?
- *Why* did the learner learn?
- *How* did the learner learn?
- *What* appeared to help or to hinder learning?

Such questions are often used by teachers, not necessarily to obtain definitive answers, but primarily for the purpose of gathering information which will provide an evidence base to aid assessment, evaluation and planning. The technique involves scrutinising the observation transcript and using these questions to select examples of, for instance, 'what the learner learned'. The sharing of views, and the analysis of data, with colleagues can help to clarify the observer's perceptions of activities within the classroom and to determine teaching approaches. This data can also provide information about the emotional, social, psychological and even physical, as well as the academic, development of pupils. The study aimed to provide teachers with an example of a teacher-friendly, manageable, dynamic, holistic model of assessment, using unstructured observation.

Choosing the children

Of the six children, with special educational needs, chosen for the study, three were taught by the second author and three were not; all were selected from Years Three, Four and Six. The selection was made in order to compare the behaviours of the children in the author's class (who had been referred) with a group of their peers who, although of a similar level of ability, had not been referred for extra help. The choice of the three children who were not taught by the author was easier to make as it was possible to use the results of a school-wide reading test which had been carried out for the local authority and had been used as an indicator of 'special need' within all primary schools in the area in order to allocate 'learning support time' to each school. Children from the same year groups, with the lowest reading scores, were placed in a parallel group. Two of these children, who had not been referred for extra help, had lower reading scores than their peers who *were* receiving extra help. The information from the observations of these children was to be used by their teachers to identify important differences in their classroom behaviours. Each pupil was observed for three different lessons, each of at least half-an-hour, as it was seen as important to observe pupils during different lessons in order to gain as full a picture as possible of their behaviours across a range of subjects and learning environments.

Recording

1) In order to reduce the degree of subjectivity, it was essential to attempt to record as much as possible of what happened. This was, and always is, difficult if not impossible, as it is obviously an enormous task to see and record everything or to know what may have been missed. A further problem is that all observers bring to the process their own distinctive perspectives which will affect what is recorded. If anything that appears to be routine or unimportant in a child's behaviour, such as sharpening a pencil or sitting awkwardly on a chair, is left out, the observer may not record actions which might assume significance during the analysis, especially if they have been repeated either regularly or spasmodically. Such behaviours may help to explain other classroom behaviours or a child's attitude to the work in progress.

2) Recording everything as it happens *without interpreting* is very difficult but, at this stage in the process, it is essential not to guess or invent thoughts behind an action. It would, for example, be misleading if it was assumed that a child who was observed going up to talk to the teacher was necessarily asking for help with a piece of work unless the actual conversation was overheard. The child might be asking for permission to go to the toilet. Another example of misinterpretation might be the assumption that because a child was frowning, that he or she did not know what to do. There could be a connection but concrete evidence is essential before any analysis is undertaken.

The observations should read like a play text:

(*John shook his head*)
MARY. Try again John, I'm sure you can do it.
(*She hands him the ball*)

Statements such as, 'I think John is upset', should not be made as they are inferences which are not based on observable evidence unless supported by a statement such as, 'John is crying'. Sentences which begin with, 'I think', 'It seems' or 'Maybe' should, therefore, be avoided, and the following form used:

(*John is still not looking at Mary...he is not responding to her questions and comments... he is staring at the floor*)

3) As previously stated, it is also important to record the *circumstances* surrounding an observed behaviour in order that, at the analysis stage, the most accurate interpretation can be obtained. For example, recording that a child is out of his seat many times during the observation period reveals very little unless the circumstances are also noted in order that possible reasons for the behaviour can be formulated at the analysis stage. The child may move about in order to sharpen a pencil, talk to others, annoy others or simply, as in one of the observations in the study, stretch his legs when he is unable to continue with a piece of work. Some might be considered legitimate activities; others could be construed as 'time wasting' or 'mischief making'.

4) Also, careful consideration should be given to the positioning of the observer and to the way in which his or her presence is explained to the observed and to the rest of the class. It also has to be decided whether the views of the learner about the learning experience should be part of the assessment procedure. The answers to questions about why an activity was or was not enjoyed can be invaluable.

5) The process of recording as much of what happens *as it happens* with pencil and paper is difficult and requires practice, although it is perhaps preferable to audio or video recording, which can be intrusive and may significantly affect the ways in which the observed behave. Nevertheless, during the study it was possible to record almost everything that happened in each case and to take note of the setting, the lesson format and the groupings; the only omissions were the occasional pupil to pupil or pupil to teacher conversations which took place out of earshot.

The study under consideration contains records of a Year Six child who appeared to be doing nothing for the first twenty minutes after the ongoing work had been explained by the teacher. She was quiet and went unnoticed. At the analysis stage of the observations, her behaviour could have been interpreted as 'daydreaming' or 'being lazy' if the full context and the dialogue between her and a friend had not also been recorded. She had, in fact, been absent during the previous lesson when the ongoing work had been started and she had failed to point this out to the head teacher who was deputising for her usual class teacher. Instead, she sat biting her nails looking worried. Eventually, after twenty minutes, she told her friend that she did not know what to do as she had been absent. Such an example indicates the benefits of systematic, unstructured observation for both teachers and pupils.

The results and analysis

The analysis of data was time-consuming owing to the amount of information from eighteen observations of approximately half-an-hour each and, in order to make them manageable, the data for each child were arranged in recurring behaviour patterns, although one-off behaviours were not discounted.

First level analysis

A summary list of behaviours, such as yawning, talking to other pupils, teacher initiated contacts with the pupil, pupil initiated contacts with the teacher, and playing with pencils or rubbers, was made, in addition to a record of occasions when the child seemed to be on task. The frequency of any behaviour was included in the summary list which was slightly different for each child as the categories were determined by what was actually observed.

Once the summary lists of the raw data of behaviours were completed, it became possible to offer explanations or interpretations. For instance, at least two explanations were possible for the behaviour of a child who was rocking from side to side and yawning while sitting on the carpet with the rest of the class and, supposedly, listening to instructions from the teacher. His behaviour may have been due to tiredness and boredom (as suggested by his frequent yawning) or to his generally observed inability to listen to and to understand information other than on a one-to-one basis, as evidenced from other data. The particular behaviour occurred during another lesson, when the children were sitting on the carpet to listen to the teacher, but was not seen during the third observation period when no one sat on the carpet at the beginning of the lesson.

Second level analysis

Once the individual lesson observations of a pupil had been analysed, recurring patterns of behaviour, or anomalies between observations, were noted in order to determine if certain behaviours occurred in every lesson or only during particular types of lessons or classroom interactions. The summaries of the interpretations of the behaviours of each child led to the formulation of cross-observational categories or categories of behaviours recorded during more than one observation. For example, one child spent most of the time during two observations doing, or appearing to do, very little except looking around the class. During the third observation, however, he was enthusiastically on task throughout. It may be that he was very tired on the first two occasions but not on the third, or that he was having difficulties with the written tasks and felt able, and therefore more motivated, to complete the practical tasks during the third observation. In addition, his animated facial expression was in stark contrast to his yawning and glazed expression during the first two observations.

Third level analysis

Two children in each year group studied, were compared across observational categories. For example, the two Year Six children talked with other pupils about both work related and non-work related subjects for a similar amount of time during the observations; both got out of their seats and also spent a similar amount of time on task. The main differences, however, between the two children (one referred and one not-referred for special help) were that the referred child constantly moved around, whereas the non-referred child sat very still and appeared to do nothing for some periods of time. The referred child initiated more than twice as many contacts with the teacher as the non-referred child and also exhibited many off task, and generally inappropriate behaviours, such as singing loudly, hitting other children and being 'silly', whereas the non-referred child exhibited none of these behaviours.

Fourth level analysis

The last level of analysis compared the referred and the non-referred groups in order to determine whether any major patterns of behaviours were common to some or all of the children within each group and whether there were any significant differences between the groups.

Table 5.1 Analysis of observed behaviours

Behaviour specific to the referred group	Behaviour common to both groups	Behaviour specific to the non-referred group
• Made and received many contacts with their teacher. • Displayed behaviours which made them very visible, e.g. fidgeting, sitting inappropriately, talking loudly and interfering with other pupils.	• Talking to peers about work and non-work subjects. • Work outcomes and time on task were similar.	• Made and received few contacts with their class teacher. • Spent periods of time sitting and appearing to be doing nothing. • Were quiet and not very visible in their behaviours, e.g. talking to their peers.

The follow-up discussions

When unstructured observation is used on a regular basis, those involved usually become more proficient at observing and the amount of information gathered about the learner is greater and more useful to all concerned, including the learner, his or her parents and the teacher. Unstructured observation works well when pairs of teachers act as reciprocal observers, each observing the other's class, and tends to build up trust and to develop sensitivity.

Whatever techniques for analysis are used, the essential aim of follow-up discussions is to increase understanding of the nature of the observed teaching and learning without judging the performance of those involved. It is essential, in reciprocal observation, for the person who is being observed to be given the opportunity to focus on what he or she feels is important before others are invited to comment. The discussion, therefore, aims to elaborate and to clarify. Elaboration is concerned with building on ideas which have been put forward, an example of which would be someone recollecting details of tasks, courses or literature relevant to the situation under discussion. Discussions should also provide information about learner achievements in the broadest, and not the academic, sense. The transcript could be dated, contextualised (as a whole or with key parts extracted), copied and included in an assessment portfolio.

The implications of the findings

The referred children maintained a high profile throughout the observations by demanding teacher attention and by their distinctive behaviours. This extra teacher attention may, in part, have been due to the teachers' awareness of the children's learning difficulties and their attempts to pre-empt misbehaviours. Consequently, the children asked for teacher help and attention and received it, and the teachers themselves initiated many more contacts with them than with the non-referred group. In contrast, the *invisible* children from the non-referred group kept a low profile and were undemanding and less noticeable in their off task behaviours. These findings are endorsed by Moses (1982) in a study of teacher assessment of children, where it was found that teachers are influenced by behaviour patterns. They associated low work rates and fidgeting with slow learning children, although children who did not exhibit such behaviours, but who were shown in tests to be slow learners, were often *not* identified as having special educational needs.

The local authority, in which the study was undertaken, allocates learning support time to schools partly on the basis of an infrequent reading test, but it was clear that in this particular school, and possibly in others, children are not assessed as having special educational needs solely on the basis of their reading ability. As two of the three non-referred children in the study had lower reading test results than their peers in the referred group, it seems possible that the teachers were using a more complex set of criteria, possibly without realising it, in order to ensure that the children *were* referred for special help. The criteria may have included the child's classroom behaviour and its effects on teachers and on other pupils, and it is possible that children who were equally in need of special help were not being referred, primarily because they did not exhibit challenging behaviour in the classroom and consequently their difficulties were underestimated.

Ways forward

The study has demonstrated that in-depth observations of pupils over an extended period can reveal previously unknown, but important, information about individuals and about groups of children and may help to clarify and quantify existing knowledge or even call into question previously held ideas about a child. The results can be used to produce an accurate account of a child's expected, and unexpected, actual behaviour in class. One unexpected finding was the extent to which the non-referred children seemed to avoid asking for help, while their peers actively sought help or attention even when they did not need it. The result was often a marked difference in teacher-pupil contacts.

Some observations may challenge a teacher's perceptions of how successfully a child is actually working. One teacher, when interviewed, believed that a child was very hard working, whereas observations showed that she sat passively and quietly doing nothing for long periods. Although another teacher stated that one child was always out of his seat and rarely on task, compared with the parallel child in the study, observations indicated that the statement was inaccurate as both children spent approximately the same time out of their seats and on task. Possibly one child's behaviours were more *noticeable*.

Recording and summarising data is not an end in itself and it is necessary to analyse the reasons or possible reasons for behaviours, and to use data diagnostically in order to understand how a child is or is not learning. The teacher can then be helped to plan more effectively and to ensure that the learning environment impacts positively on the child.

The Code of Practice on the Identification and Assessment of Special Educational Needs (DfE 1994) requires more detailed information about a child's strengths and weaknesses for the preparation of largely formative and diagnostic individual education plans, in contrast with the previous summative records of achievement. Detailed observations provide useful data on factors which influence:

- how a child works best;
- what a child's learning strategies might be in other situations;
- how a child is affected by different environments and styles of teaching;
- how a child interacts with his or her peers.

There are also advantages in trying to include a short debriefing, with the child observed and with the teacher, in order to elicit views on how the child worked during the lesson, although in the study, it was not possible with each child on every occasion.

Using observation

Although detailed unstructured observation can be problematical for class teachers, it is possible for learning support teachers to undertake such activities. Alternatively, class teachers could, if they have non-contact time, observe children in other teachers' classes and thus provide valuable and more objective insights into the relationships between class teachers and their pupils. An interesting example of the process occurred during a study of a child who appeared to have a strong teacher-dependent attitude and who would not do anything without expecting personal individual instruction from a particular teacher. He tended to follow her around until he received the attention he sought and, in addition, he received many teacher initiated contacts. He was later observed while being taught by another teacher and the contrast between the behaviours observed was striking. He did not seek the second teacher's attention and he received few teacher initiated contacts, despite appearing to be uncertain of what was expected of him, as evidenced by a lengthy spell of 'doing nothing'. He seemed to actively avoid contact with the second teacher and it would appear that his dependent relationship was specific to the first teacher. Such differences in his behaviour are unlikely to have been so clearly illustrated in the absence of observation.

Nevertheless, in schools with limited resources, particularly those in the primary sector, teachers are unlikely to have sufficient non-contact time to undertake such an exercise. There are also other possible ways forward. As a child study is a requirement on many primary PGCE and BEd courses, students could be used as observers or, alternatively while they are in schools on teaching practice they could free staff to observe other classes.

Observation techniques might be further developed by focusing either on specific areas of the curriculum which a school felt were in need of improvement or on year groups with particular difficulties. Alternatively, particular children could be observed periodically over more than one academic year in order to chart progress and development with different teachers. Additionally, class teachers could observe children over an extended period to discover ways of improving specific areas of class organisation in order to benefit the whole class and not only those children with learning difficulties. Teachers constantly observe children when teaching, but a more formal commitment to systematic, recorded observation of certain children or areas of the curriculum could be a tool for reflection and professional development.

Using observation as a means of discovering how children behave in class has demonstrated the factors which impinge on, and affect, the learning process for all children, but especially for those with learning difficulties. One example of the effect of the environment upon a learner was the child who was often out of his seat seeking the attention of the teacher and the children around him. An analysis of the data showed that he could not see the blackboard from his position against a wall, where he had been placed to keep him in his seat. The observation also showed that he got up and wandered around when he was unable to continue his work and was unwilling to ask for help. If his wandering was to be stopped, the seating had to be rearranged and he had to be persuaded to put up his hand to ask for help. Withdrawing children for specific help can be a valid means of achieving learning goals and even with limited time it can be effective. Nevertheless, changes in the classroom environment are usually even more effective and long-lasting.

This study indicated that open-ended ethnographic observation, such as unstructured observation, can provide surprising insights into how children work and interact in the classroom and can lead to significant professional development for the teachers involved. It can also be used as an integral part of dynamic assessment, eliciting data which leads to more accurate assessments of ongoing learning of all types over a period of time.

References

Cohen, R., Hughes, M.. with Ashworth, L. and Blair, M. (1994) *School's Out! The Family Perspective on School Exclusion*. London: Barnardos and Family Service Units.

Delamont, S. and Hamilton, D. (1983) 'Classroom research: a critique and a new approach to Interaction Analysis', in Stubbs, M. and Delamont, S. (eds) *Explorations in Classroom Observation*. Bath: Wiley.

Department of Education and Science (1981) *Education Act*. London: HMSO.

Department of Education and Science (1988) *Education Reform Act 1988*. London: DES.

Drummond, M. J. (1993) *Assessing Children's Learning*. London: David Fulton Publishers.

Fish, J. and Evans, J. (1995) *Managing Special Education: Codes, Charters and Competition*. Milton Keynes: Open University Press.

Flanders, N. (1964) 'Some relationships among teachers influence pupil attitudes and achievement', in Biddle, B. and Ellena, W. J. (eds) *Contemporary Research on Teacher Effectiveness*. New York: Holt, Rhinehart and Winston.

Fletcher-Campbell, F. (1996) *The Resourcing of Special Educational Needs*. Slough: NFER.

Fletcher-Campbell, F. and Lee, B. (1995) *Effective Assessment where Pupils Make Small Steps of Progress in the National Curriculum* (Final Report for SCAA). Slough: NFER.

Fogell, J. and Long, R. (1997) *Emotional and Behavioural Difficulties*. Tamworth: NASEN Publications.

Galton, M. (1978) *British Mirrors: a Collection of Classroom Observation*

Systems. Leicester: University of Leicester, School of Education.

Glaser, B. G. and Strauss, A. L. (1967) *The Discovery of Grounded Theory Strategies for Qualitative Research*. Chicago: Aldine.

Goacher, B., Evans, J., Welton, J. and Wedell, K. (1988) *Policy and Provision for Special Educational Needs: Implementing the 1981 Education Act*. London: Cassell.

Goldbart, J. (1994) 'Opening the communication curriculum to students with PMLDs', in Ware, J. (ed.) *Educating Children with Profound and Multiple Learning Difficulties*. London: David Fulton Publishers.

Lloyd-Smith, M. and Dwyfor Davies, J. (1995) *On the Margins*. Stoke-on-Trent: Trentham Books.

Moses, D. (1982) 'Special educational needs: the relationship between teacher assessment, test scores and classroom behaviour', *British Education Research Journal* **8** (2), 111–22.

Office of Her Majesty's Chief Inspector of Schools (1997) *The SEN Code of Practice: Two Years On*. London: OFSTED.

Schools Curriculum and Assessment Authority (1996) *Planning the Curriculum for Pupils with Profound and Multiple Learning Difficulties*. London: SCAA.

Stakes, R. and Hornby, G. (1996) *Meeting Special Needs in Mainstream Schools*. London: David Fulton Publishers.

Walker, R. and Adelman, C. (1975) *A Guide to Classroom Observation Systems*. London: Methuen.

Ware, J. (ed.) *Educating Children with Profound and Multiple Learning Difficulties*. London: David Fulton Publishers.

Ware, J. and Healey, I. (1994) 'Conceptualizing progress in children with profound and multiple learning difficulties', in Ware, J. (ed.) *Educating Children with Profound and Multiple Learning Difficulties*. London: David Fulton Publishers.

Chapter 6

From Observation to Inference about Challenging Behaviours

John Harris

Introduction

Children with severe learning difficulties present a number of challenges to teachers:

- the creation of a curriculum which is 'broad, balanced and relevant to their needs' (Ashdown *et al.* 1991; Carpenter *et al.* 1996);
- communication with children who have a limited ability to understand and use spoken language (Harris and Wimpory 1993);
- additional cognitive, sensory and physical impairments which are likely to have adverse effects on their development and learning.

Together these challenges make both accurate assessment and effective teaching a complex and demanding task.

Challenging behaviour is an additional obstacle to effective teaching. Nevertheless, unlike physical or sensory impairment, it is not a quality or personal characteristic which pupils *carry around* with them and neither is it a direct outcome of an underlying medical condition. The challenge presented by problem behaviours needs to be seen in a wider context, framed by: schools which are committed to a range of educational objectives; a curriculum which reflects the needs of a broad population of students; a form of organisation which commits one or two adults to work with a group of eight to ten pupils; and teachers who have been trained in a particular pedagogic tradition. It is the interaction between pupils (whose intellectual abilities are severely impaired) and the environments (in which they live and learn) that creates challenging behaviours. These interactions provide the focus for describing and making sense of challenging behaviours.

The identification of challenging behaviours

Challenging behaviours are easy to recognise but rather more difficult to define and to measure. The three issues of identification, measurement and definition are therefore addressed separately, beginning with the relatively straightforward one of identification. In general, teachers find it fairly easy to identify which pupils and which behaviours currently present a challenge, and studies which have documented teachers' responses indicate a considerable degree of consensus on what kinds of behaviour present a challenge in the classroom (Harris *et al.* 1996; Kiernan and Kiernan 1994). For example, in response to a postal survey of 33 special schools in the West Midlands, Harris *et al.* (1996) report the following list of behaviours rated as severely challenging:

- physical aggression towards others;
- self-injury;
- distracting others/hyperactivity;
- shouting/swearing/loud noises;
- damage to property;
- obsessive and ritualistic behaviour;
- non-compliance;
- disruption/interference with work in the classroom;
- behaviours that put the safety of self or others at risk;
- inappropriate sexual behaviour;
- incontinence/soiling/smearing;
- self-stimulation, including masturbation;
- spitting;
- running away;
- tantrums;
- throwing objects.

The list is interesting for a number of reasons. Firstly, the behaviours have a strong element of face validity and most people would agree that they would be inappropriate in the classroom. Secondly, closer inspection suggests that these are not neat categories but intuitive attempts to capture the features of different behaviours which put them in the *challenging* category. As a result, some items, such as 'disruption', represent a description of the effect or outcome of the behaviour rather than the actions performed by the pupil (Harris *et al.* 1996; Lowe and Felce 1995). There is also considerable overlap between descriptions; for example, damaging property and throwing things, or ritualistic behaviours and non-compliance (these behaviours are often recognised as ritualistic when pupils do not comply with requests which would interrupt the ritual). This raises the important question of how far these descriptions reflect a consistent interpretation of what counts (or does not count) as challenging behaviour. Thirdly, the descriptions provide no information on *why* the behaviours occur. Before addressing concerns about the definition of challenging behaviour, and looking more closely at why challenging behaviours occur, it is worthwhile to consider one of the advantages which immediately arises from the identification of behaviours which challenge.

From identification to measurement

One of the factors which determines the impact of challenging behaviours is the level at which they occur. 'Level' may refer to how often the behaviour occurs (its frequency), how long it lasts (its duration), or how much energy it absorbs (its intensity) (see Chapter 2). Behaviours which occur at a high frequency, with a long duration or with high intensity, are more likely to be regarded as challenging than those which do not. For example, compare the pupil who tries to pinch the person next to him about once a week, with the child who performs the same behaviour every five minutes; the pupil who runs around the classroom for the first few minutes of a lesson, with the child who does this for the whole lesson; the child who pats his head with his hand, and the child who slaps his head with great force. When a challenging behaviour has been identified, it is possible, using the methods described in Chapter 2, to measure the overall strength of the behaviour in an objective way.

However, while the terms set out above refer to behaviours, they would all require a more precise behavioural description before they could be used as a basis for observational measurement. For example, in the study by Harris *et al.* (1996), Adam demonstrated physical aggression by biting and scratching other pupils, while for Michael, physical aggression took the form of shouting at other people while jabbing his forefinger into the middle of the other person's chest. The topography of physical aggression is different for these two children and any attempt at measuring aggression (or any other type of behaviour) should focus on the precise descriptions of individual behaviours. An additional complication is that most pupils who challenge do so with a number of different behaviours. Harris *et al.* (1996) provide a good example:

> Clive constantly flaps his hands in front of his face and around his groin; he makes loud noises, screams, stamps his feet and bangs doors, tables and walls with his hands. He sometimes grabs staff and

sinks his nails into their hands. He regularly twirls around rapidly
while standing in one place.

(p.65)

Clive's obsessive and ritualistic behaviours include flapping his hands in
front of his face and twirling around while standing in one place. He also
displays aggression towards other people (sinking his nails into the hands of
staff), and self-injury, (banging doors, tables and walls with his hands). Clive
was initially identified as presenting disruptive behaviour, aggression,
obsessive and ritualistic behaviours and self-injury. However, for the purposes of measurement, he displays seven distinct behavioural topographies.

Table 6.1

Terms used for identification	Behaviours which can be measured
Aggression	sinks nails into hands of staff
Obsessive/ritualistic behaviours	flapping hands in front of face
	flapping hands around groin
	twirling round while standing in one place
Self-injury	banging doors, tables and walls with one hand
Disruption	making noises and screaming
	stamping feet

This approach to the measurement of challenging behaviour involves
recording each occurrence of a particular behaviour over a period of time
using the methods described in Chapter 2. An alternative methodology is
based on the idea that specific challenging behaviours are indicators or
symptoms of a more general underlying disorder. From this perspective,
the aim of description is to identify, in a reliable way, the *underlying
problem* or disorder on the basis of the particular pattern of challenging
behaviours. Accurate measurement of frequency, duration and intensity of
specific behaviours is less important than a comprehensive picture of the
range of different behaviours which any individual child presents. Various
observation schedules and checklists have been developed to assist record
keeping and to ensure that children are reliably assigned to clinical
categories on the basis of their behaviours (see Chapter 3).

A good example of a checklist of behaviours which can be used with
pupils with severe learning disabilities is the *Nisonger Child Behaviour
Rating Form* (N-CBRF) currently being developed by Aman *et al.* (1996).
Parallel forms for parents and teachers invite an adult, who knows the
child well, to indicate whether or not each of 66 problem behaviours

occurred 'occasionally', 'quite often' or 'a lot'. Scores can then be generated for six sub-scales to indicate the behavioural category which best describes the child. Examples of behaviours which are associated with different types of *problem* are shown in Table 6.2.

Table 6.2 (adapted from Aman *et al.* 1996)

Underlying problem:	Behaviour:
Conduct problem	defiant: challenges adult authority knowingly destroys property disobedient gets into physical fights
Insecure/anxious	exaggerates abilities or achievements feels others are against him or her feels worthless or inferior lying or cheating
Hyperactive	difficulty concentrating easily distracted fails to finish things that he has started fidgets, wriggles or squirms
Self-injury/Stereotypy	hits or slaps own head, neck, hands or other body parts rocks body or head back and forth repetitively harms self by scratching skin or pulling hair gouges self, puts things in ears, nose etc. or eats inedible things
Self-isolated/Ritualistic	apathetic or unmotivated has rituals such as head rolling or floor pacing shy around others; bashful isolates self from others
Overly sensitive	clings to adults, too dependent crying, tearful episodes easily frustrated overly sensitive; feelings easily hurt

How can challenging behaviour be defined?

A definition of challenging behaviour would be helpful for a number of reasons. Teachers would find it easier to distinguish behaviours which challenge from those which are merely irritating or inconvenient, and the measurement of challenging behaviour would be placed on a firmer footing. A definition would help to ensure that teachers working with different pupils in different schools adopted a consistent approach to the identification of challenging behaviours and it would make it much easier to determine the number of children who present challenging behaviours in relation to characteristics such as age, sex and disability.

However, a satisfactory definition of challenging behaviour has proved difficult to achieve because the concept of 'challenging' is based upon a number of factors over and above the precise nature of the behaviour. Determinants of challenging behaviour include:

- *Culture*, the extent to which behavioural and verbal expressions of aggression are tolerated varies across cultures;
- *Age*, stamping and banging fists on the table in response to frustration may be tolerated in a toddler, but might be regarded as challenging when carried out by a fifteen-year-old;
- *Context*, running is likely to be encouraged in the school playground, but regarded as disruptive in the classroom;
- *Antecedents*, hitting another child will be judged as unacceptable aggression, unless there is a reasonable justification, such as the other child hitting out first;
- *Long-term consequences*, withdrawal from social contact may be as regarded as challenging because of the reduced opportunities for learning and future placement which it entails.

All of these factors are relevant to judgements about behaviours which challenge, but there is no formula which can be used to determine unambiguously what behaviours *count* and what behaviours *do not count* as challenging. The best that can be achieved is a concise summary of the factors which should be taken into consideration when making a judgement on whether or not a behaviour is to be considered challenging. Emerson (1995) offers the following:

> Culturally abnormal behaviours of such an intensity, frequency or duration that the physical safety of the person or others is likely to be placed in serious jeopardy, or behaviour which is likely to seriously limit the use of, or result in the person being denied access to, ordinary community facilities.

(pp.4–5)

Similarly, Harris *et al.* (1996) asked teachers to select pupils for participation in their study who presented behaviours which met the following criteria:

93

- prevented participation in educational activities;
- isolated pupils from their peers;
- affected the learning of other pupils;
- drastically reduced opportunities for involvement in ordinary community activities;
- made excessive demands on staff and other resources;
- placed the child or other pupils in physical danger;
- threatened the prospect of future placement.

Beyond measurement

Identification and measurement are essential first steps in addressing the needs of pupils who present challenging behaviours. However, on their own they do little to address the more fundamental question of why challenging behaviour occurs. The search for an explanation about the cause of challenging behaviour leads on to a more detailed approach to observation and a more elaborate descriptive framework.

Very often challenging behaviours are established, and subsequently maintained, in the face of the best efforts of family members and schools to reduce the extent to which they occur. Challenging behaviours of sufficient intensity, frequency or duration are regarded in terms of Emerson's definition as 'serious', having proved resistant to the usual forms of parental discipline and to educational methods employed by teachers. There are a number of reasons why this is less surprising than it might first appear. Firstly, when they initially appear, behaviours which subsequently pose a major challenge may seem benign or insignificant and it is only when they have become relatively well established that they are recognised as posing serious problems (Murphy and Oliver 1987). Secondly, the factors which motivate challenging behaviours among children with severe learning disabilities may be different from those which motivate non-disabled children (Reiss and Havercamp 1997). For example, twirling and flapping by pupils with autistic spectrum disorders may help to regulate the child's level of stimulation, and social contact may be a source of anxiety and stress rather than comfort and reassurance (Frith 1989). Similarly, for some children, self-injury provides an automatic reinforcement (Repp *et al.* 1988; Winchel and Stanley 1991). Thirdly, there is some evidence to suggest that problem behaviours presented by children with learning disabilities elicit reactions from adults which are different from those which occur in response to similar behaviour by non-disabled children (Carr *et al.* 1991; Cuskelly and Dadds 1992). Fourthly, few children who present challenging behaviours have the linguistic abilities and the degree of insight needed for them to explain why they display challenging behaviours (Kiernan and Kiernan 1994). Overall, it is far from surprising that conventional classroom practices and insights derived from working with non-disabled pupils often fail to illuminate explanations about causes or suggest strategies for responding to severely challenging behaviours among pupils with severe learning disabilities.

An alternative response has been to adopt a rigorous approach to observation, record keeping and the analysis of data as the most effective way of addressing a fundamental question about the causes of human behaviour: what are the benefits and costs for the child of performing the behaviour in particular circumstances? Without the opportunity to benefit from personal introspection, the only way to answer this question is to examine the relationship between specific behaviours and changes in the environment. This is the domain of functional analysis. The benefits of this approach are that it sweeps away preconceptions about what is reasonable or plausible in terms of our own experience, and seeks to establish relationships objectively using scientific methods. The factors which might be examined by a thorough functional analysis, are:

- *Antecedent environmental factors*, including the overall level of stimulation (e.g. working in a very noisy classroom compared to a one-to-one teaching session in an empty room) and specific events, such as being instructed to undertake a particular task, or the arrival of the school bus;
- *Contingent environmental events* which occur after a behaviour. For example, attention in response to self-injury, or the provision of an alternative, less demanding, curriculum activity;
- *Motivational state of the pupil*. For example, he might be particularly sensitive or unusually unresponsive to stimulation, depending upon illness, hunger, a lack of sleep, or the use of medication.

Until recently, functional analysis has focused upon elucidating the relationship between challenging behaviours and their antecedents and consequences, with relatively little attention having been given to motivational status.

Functional analysis

A robust functional analysis would consider all necessary and sufficient conditions to explain the occurrence of a behaviour and to demonstrate

95

these relationships empirically (Oliver and Head 1993). An outline procedure for a functional analysis using observational procedures will:

1. Describe the behaviour in order that it can be measured in terms of frequency, duration and intensity.
2. Identify the environmental events or conditions which consistently precede the occurrence of the behaviour.
3. Identify events which consistently follow the behaviour.
4. Generate hypotheses about relationships which could explain the occurrence of the behaviour.
5. Manipulate key environmental events to demonstrate empirically that the relationship exists.

However, the difficulties posed by adhering to these principles in applied settings mean that these standards are rarely achieved in practice.

Steps 2 and 3 are most effectively carried out using systematic direct observations as described in Chapter 2. Nevertheless, this is an extremely time intensive procedure, even if only one pupil is involved and, for this reason, alternative procedures have been developed. For example, after a period of classroom observation in partnership with teachers and their assistants, Harris *et al.* (1996) invited teachers to participate in a review meeting which was structured around five questions about the pupil's challenging behaviour:

- How do you think the situation, in which the challenging behaviour occurs, appears to N?
- How are present strategies helping?
- What problems are associated with the present strategies?
- How do you think N's needs can be met?
- What structures need to be in place in school for N's needs to be met?

The first question was deliberately designed to encourage teachers and classroom assistants to move away from thinking about the problems which the behaviour created in relation to their attempts to organise classroom activities, and to consider, instead, what would motivate the pupil to perform that particular challenging behaviour. An alternative approach to identifying functional relationships, using the experience of adults who know the child well, is the Motivational Assessment Scale, a 16-item rating scale used to help staff to identify the factors associated with challenging behaviours (Durand 1990). The scale concentrates on four motivational categories, which have been found to be consistently associated with challenging behaviours. These are listed in Table 6.3

together with examples of questions which are designed to indicate whether or not the motive is operative.

Table 6.3 (from Durand 1990)

Motivation	Question from Motivational Assessment Scale (MAS)
• Boredom	Would the behaviour occur continuously, over and over, if this person was left alone for long periods of time? (For example, for several hours)
• Task avoidance	Does the behaviour occur following a request to perform a difficult task?
• Attention seeking	Does the behaviour seem to occur in response to your talking to other persons in the room?
• Attaining tangible reinforcement	Does the behaviour ever occur when you take away a favourite toy, food or activity?

While the MAS is far less accurate than direct observation, it provides a relatively quick and reliable method of exploring functional relationships and is likely to be of particular value to staff who lack the expertise or the time needed for undertaking observational studies (Durand and Crimmins 1988).

Demonstrating empirical relationships

A functional analysis should lead to one or more hypotheses about the causes of a challenging behaviour (Repp *et al.* 1988), which may be tested empirically in one of three different ways. First, the method of direct observation may be used in conjunction with systematic manipulations of environmental variables. For example, if it is suspected that the motivation for a behaviour is the avoidance of a specific task or activity, this can be tested by observing the occurrence of the behaviour during intervals when the task is presented and when it is not. Importantly, care should be taken to ensure that all other antecedent and consequent environmental variables are unchanged.

Secondly, it is possible to test out a number of specific hypotheses by placing the pupil in settings which have been artificially created to elicit particular motivational states. Such settings are often referred to as 'analogues' of the functional relationships which occur in real life settings. For example, Iwata *et al.* (1990) created settings to test predicted relationships between self-injury and three motivational states: attention seeking; demand avoidance; automatic reinforcement. Each of the three settings was designed to provide specific antecedent conditions or contingent events following the occurrence of self-injury. A third control condition involved free play.

Table 6.4

Hypothesised motivation	Environmental design
• Attention seeking	Adult directs participant toward play materials and then reads a magazine. Contingent on occurrence of Self-injurious behaviour (SIB),adult approaches, expresses concern, or disapproval, and gives brief physical contact or comfort.
• Demand avoidance	Specially selected tasks are presented in learning trials with a response required about once every thirty seconds. Correct responses are followed by praise while incorrect responses are followed by modelling a correct response and, if necessary, physically prompting the child's response. Contingent on occurrence of SIB, the trial is terminated, materials are then removed and the adult ignores the participant.
• Automatic reinforcement	A 'barren' environment in which SIB might occur if motivated by boredom.

In this study, all seven participants displayed the highest levels of self-injury in the demand condition.

The third way in which possible functional relationships can be tested is by introducing a form of intervention specifically designed to reduce or ameliorate the challenging behaviour. The major limitations of this approach are, firstly, that if interventions are to be maximally effective, they will involve a number of different components which may preclude testing out a specific relationship. Secondly, a convincing demonstration that the intervention was successful, because it targeted a particular functional relation, would require a temporary removal of the intervention procedures after an initial reduction in the challenging behaviour. A consequent increase in the level of the challenging behaviour would confirm the initial hypothesis about the causes of the behaviour. For ethical reasons, such procedures are rarely used in practice. While it will be abundantly evident when an intervention has failed (continuing high levels of challenging behaviour), the *reasons* for the failure may be less obvious. It may be that the presumed motivational basis for the challenging behaviour was incorrect, or that the intervention was poorly targeted or inconsistently applied. Even where the intervention seems to be effective, there may be other unknown factors which contribute to (or even cause) positive outcomes.

Notwithstanding the complexity of the procedures employed, a functional analysis is the preferred method of identifying the causes of challenging behaviours for a number of reasons:

- it clearly distinguishes between interpretations based upon subjective or intuitive judgements and those derived from the application of a scientific method;
- it encourages a broad range of hypotheses, not simply those which fit with preconceptions about particular children;
- because functional analysis is based upon data, it encourages a systematic examination of the behaviour;
- it includes a method for choosing between alternative hypotheses about possible causes;
- it helps to explain behaviour which would otherwise remain inexplicable;
- it suggests ways of reducing challenging behaviours by manipulating environmental variables.

Communication and challenging behaviour

Functional analysis has helped to demonstrate the wide range of causal events which can lead to challenging behaviour. Nevertheless, analogue assessments such as those developed by Iwata *et al.* (1990) and interview methods such as the MAS are based upon the finding that many challenging behaviours occur in response to a small number of motivational states, such as boredom, task avoidance, or attempts to escape from a situation which is unpleasant or distressing. An additional motivational state which is increasingly identified with challenging behaviours is communication.

The idea that challenging behaviour is essentially an attempt to communicate is an exciting hypothesis, based upon different types of evidence, such as the role of non-verbal behaviour in the development of communication (see Harris 1990) and research which indicates that among people with a learning disability, those with poor communication skills have higher rates of challenging behaviours. Interestingly, behavioural research has developed a definition of communication based upon the responses of other people rather than the intentions of the child responsible for the behaviour. For example, Wacker *et al.* (1990) worked with Bobby, a child with autism and severe learning disability who bit his hand several times an hour and often drew blood. Assessment (using three analogue conditions; escape from demands, tangible reinforcement, and social attention) indicated that hand biting was maintained by positive reinforcement, and this relationship was used as the basis for treatment. Using positive reinforcement, Bobby was taught to perform a non-challenging behaviour, (lightly touching or brushing his chin) and, in the second phase of treatment, tangible reinforcement was made contingent on this behaviour, rather than biting. During the treatment sessions, the level of challenging behaviour dropped dramatically and Bobby quickly learnt to use the non-challenging behaviour, rather than biting, to achieve his favourite reinforcer.

Not surprisingly, Wacker *et al.* (1990) refer to Bobby's non-challenging behaviour (lightly touching or brushing his chin) as a 'sign', but on what basis can the new behaviour be described as communicative? Although the adults working with Bobby have been taught to interpret 'touching or brushing his chin' as a sign meaning 'I want X', it is by no means clear that Bobby understands the communicative significance of his behaviour. Other authors (Carr and Durand 1985) suggest that it may be 'helpful to view misbehaviour *as if* it were a form of non-verbal communication, specifically, a request for certain behaviours on the part of others' (p.125; italics in original).

Functional communication training has two important advantages. It provides adults with a powerful cue for the delivery of reinforcement, contingent upon appropriate, rather than inappropriate, behaviour. For example, Carr and Durand taught children to use phrases such as 'Am I doing good work?' as a request for attention instead of challenging behaviours such as aggression or self-injury. Also, the child is given effective control over adult responses which have been shown to have reinforcing properties. However, this only occurs if functional relationships have been clearly delineated so that the new 'communicative behaviour' elicits the same class of responses which were previously responsible for maintaining the challenging behaviour (Carr and Durand 1985).

There are also three dangers associated with the communication hypothesis for challenging behaviour. The first is that it is adopted wholesale as *the* explanation for challenging behaviour and that other possible motivations such as undiagnosed pain or internal reinforcement are ignored. The second is that communicative functions will be 'diagnosed' intuitively on the basis of insufficient evidence and without a full consideration of alternatives. Once again, it is important to emphasise that the functional communication training should be based on a clear understanding of the adult responses which maintain the challenging behaviour in question.

The third danger is that the communicative competence of children with challenging behaviour will be overestimated. This occurs when the identification of functional relationships is translated into mentalistic concepts without sufficient evidence. For example, it is one thing to demonstrate that a child can be taught to use one behaviour (a sign) instead of another (self-injury) in response to the manipulation of reinforcement contingencies (adult attention). But this does no more than to suggest, as an hypothesis, the much more sophisticated interpretation, that the child engages in self-injury *in order* to achieve adult attention. For this more elaborate concept of communication to be applicable, it would also be necessary to show that the child can represent future states of affairs (teacher attention compared to no attention) and conceive of people as being distinct from objects and machines in the sense that they are motivated by beliefs, desires and feelings. Whereas there has been a great deal of interest in the difficulties children with autism experience in developing a theory of mind, there has been no comparable research with those who present challenging behaviours (Frith 1989).

Summary

This chapter has used challenging behaviour to illustrate the close relationship between observation, interpretation and intervention. While challenging behaviours are deceptively simple to recognise in classroom settings, observation, record keeping and measurement are dependent upon an objective delineation of their topographical features. Without the opportunity to ask the children themselves why they carry out such behaviours, understanding the causes of challenging behaviour requires a systematic exploration of the relationship between the behaviour and the environment in which it occurs. Motivational factors for challenging behaviour include events which precede the behaviour, the consequences which follow performance of the behaviour, and the internal states which determine the child's sensitivity to these environmental events (Reiss and Havercamp 1997).

Whereas traditional functional analysis is dependent upon extensive and robust observational data, more recent innovations have utilised reports from teachers and other adults who know the child well. Challenging behaviours have been linked to a number of distinct motivational states, including boredom, attainment of tangible reinforcers, avoidance or escape from demanding situations and adult attention. Finally, a number of intervention studies have shown children can be taught to use non-challenging behaviours, which have communicative significance for adults, instead of well established challenging behaviours. It is important to distinguish between behaviours which elicit a reinforcing adult response and behaviours which are communicative in the sense that they are predicated on an emerging set of beliefs and expectations about how and why people behave as they do. There is no evidence to suggest that challenging behaviours, in general, are indicative of more sophisticated communicative abilities which have somehow been blocked or frustrated, but this remains a potentially fruitful area for further research.

References

Aman, M. G., Tasse, M. J., Rojahn, J. and Hammer, D. (1996) *The Nisonger Child Behaviour Rating Form* (unpublished rating scale). Columbus, OH: Ohio State University.

Ashdown, R., Carpenter, B. and Bovair, K. (1991) *The Curriculum Challenge.* London: Falmer Press.

Carpenter, B., Ashdown, R. and Bovair, K. (1996) *Enabling Access.* London: David Fulton Publishers.

Carr, E. G. and Durand, V. M. (1985) 'Reducing behaviour problems through functional communication training', *Journal of Applied Behaviour Analysis* **18** (2), 111–26.

Carr, E. G., Taylor, J. C. and Robinson, S. (1991) 'The effects of severe behaviour problems in children on the teaching behaviour of adults', *Journal of Applied Behaviour Analysis* **24** (3), 523–35.

Cuskelly, M. and Dadds, M. (1992) 'Behavioural problems in children with Down's syndrome and their siblings', *Journal of Child Psychology and Psychiatry* **33** (4), 749–61.

Durand, V. M. and Crimmins, D. B. (1988) 'Identifying the variables maintaining self-injurious behaviour', *Journal of Autism and Developmental Disorders* **18** (1), 99–117.

Durand, V. M. (1990) *Severe Behaviour Problems: a Functional Communication*

Training Approach. New York: The Guilford Press.

Emerson, E. (1995) *Challenging Behaviour: Analysis and Intervention in People with Learning Difficulties*. Cambridge: Cambridge University Press.

Frith, U. (1989) *Autism: Explaining the Enigma*. Oxford: Blackwell.

Harris, J. (1990) *Early Language Development: Implications for Clinical and Educational Practice*. London: Routledge.

Harris, J., Cook, M. and Upton, G. (1996) *Pupils with Severe Learning Disabilities who Present Challenging Behaviour: a Whole School Approach to Assessment and Intervention*. Kidderminster: BILD Publications.

Harris, J., Cook, M. and Upton, G. (1993) 'Challenging behaviour in the classroom', in Harris, J. (ed.) *Innovations in Educating Children with Severe Learning Difficulties*. Chorley: Lisieux Hall.

Harris, J. and Wimpory, D. (1993) 'Encouraging early language and communication', in Harris, J. (ed.) *Innovations in Educating Children with Severe Learning Difficulties*. Chorley: Lisieux Hall.

Iwata, B. A., Pace, G. M., Kalshar, M. J., Cowdery, G. E. and Cataldo, M. F. (1990) 'Experimental analysis and extinction of self-injurious escape behaviour', *Journal of Applied Behaviour Analysis* **23** (1), 11–27.

Kiernan, C. and Kiernan, D. (1994) 'Challenging behaviour in schools for pupils with severe learning difficulties', *Mental Handicap Research* **7** (3), 177–201.

Lowe, K. and Felce, D. (1995) 'The definition of challenging behaviour in practice', *British Journal of Learning Disabilities* **23** (3), 118–23.

Murphy, G. and Oliver, C. (1987) 'Decreasing undesirable behaviour', in Yule, W. and Carr, J. (eds) *Behaviour Modification for People with Mental Handicaps*, 2nd edn. London: Croom Helm.

Oliver, C. and Head, D. (1993) 'Self-injurious behaviour: functional analysis and interventions', in Jones, R. S. P. and Eayrs, C. B. (eds) *Challenging Behaviour and Intellectual Disability: a Psychological Perspective*. Kidderminster: BILD Publications.

Reiss, S. and Havercamp, S. M. (1997) 'Sensitivity theory and mental retardation: why functional analysis is not enough', *American Journal of Mental Retardation* **101** (6), 553–66.

Repp, A. C., Felce, D. and Barton, L. E. (1988) 'Basing the treatment of stereotypic and self-injurious behaviours on the hypotheses of their causes', *Journal of Applied Behaviour Analysis* **21** (3), 281–9.

Wacker, D. P., Stegge, M. W., Northrup, G. S., Berg, W., Reimers, T., Cooper, L., Cigrand, K. and Donn, L. (1990) 'A component analysis of functional communication training across three topographies of severe behaviour problems', *Journal of Applied Behaviour Analysis* **23** (4), 417–29.

Winchel, R. M. and Stanley, M. S. (1991) 'Self-injurious behaviour: a review of the behaviour and biology of self-mutilation', *American Journal of Psychiatry* **148** (3), 306–17.

CHAPTER 7

The Role of Observation in Teacher Appraisal

John Moore

Introduction

The need for a national appraisal scheme for teachers was first discussed in Paragraph 92 of *Teaching Quality* (DES 1983). Two years later, *Better Schools* (DES 1985) laid down markers for the establishment of a national framework. Her Majesty's Inspectorate (HMI) then produced the occasional paper, *Quality in Schools: Evaluation and Appraisal* (DES 1985), which was particularly successful in focusing subsequent discussions. After a protracted period of debate, pilot studies were set up in Croydon, Cumbria, Newcastle-upon-Tyne, Salford, Somerset and Suffolk, which started in January 1987 and continued into 1989. They were overseen by a National Steering Group which recommended a national framework for head teacher and teacher appraisal. Following a period of consultation, Kenneth Clarke (Hansard, December 1990), the then Secretary of State for Education and Science, announced that the appraisal of schoolteachers should be compulsory, and therefore 'it is a duty for employers and an entitlement for teachers' (p.292). Regulations were then laid before Parliament, and *School Teacher Appraisal* (Circular 12/91, DES 1991a) was published on 24 July 1991; the scheme itself commenced in September 1991.

From the outset, classroom observation has formed an important part of the appraisal process, contributing both to professional and institutional development in the form of school improvement. It is this one aspect of appraisal more than any other, however, which has received most criticism. Nevertheless, the development of classroom observation within the appraisal cycle and its subsequent impact on classroom practice, remains a goal worthy of achievement. This chapter focuses on developments leading to the attainment of this goal.

The appraisal process in Kent

An agreement made between the teachers' professional associations and the Advisory, Conciliation and Arbitration Service (ACAS) in 1986 (*Teacher' Dispute ACAS Independent Panel* [Report of the Appraisal/Training Working Group], reproduced in DES 1989) defined appraisal as:

> ...a continuous and systematic process intended to help individual teachers with their professional development and career planning, and to help ensure that in-service training and the deployment of teachers matches the complementary needs of individual teachers and the schools.
>
> (p.1)

The Kent scheme, which was set up in 1990, reflects this definition. Kent LEA, through regular consultation and support for its head teachers and appraisal coordinators, has developed appraisal in line with the changes which have taken place in education since 1991 and has had experience of managing appraisal for 650 head teachers and approximately 10,000 teachers. One of the strengths of the scheme is its commitment to high quality training. It offers residential courses to all appraisers and recently-appointed head teachers and, in addition, all teachers have an entitlement to receive one day's training prior to appraisal. The appraisal process covers a two year cycle as Figure 7.1 illustrates.

In the Kent scheme, appraisees prepare for their appraisal by engaging in a general self-review, which enables them to identify areas of focus to be discussed at the initial meeting. Circular 12/91 (DES 1991a), Paragraph 11, requires that:

> Appraisal should be set in the context of the objectives of the schools, which will generally be expressed in the school development plan. Appraisal should support development planning and vice versa. The school's objectives in a particular year should be linked with appraisal, so that, for example, professional development targets arising from appraisal may be related to agreed tasks and targets in the development plan. Similarly, appraisal targets, when taken together, should provide an important agenda for action for the school as a whole.
>
> (p.2)

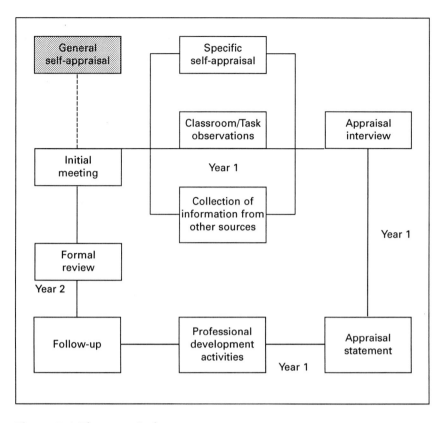

Figure 7.1 The appraisal process

In this context, appraisees consider: their current job description and whether it needs updating or changing; what has given them the greatest satisfaction; what has gone less well; modifications to the school organisation which might enhance their performance; the broad areas for change over the appraisal period; hopes and aspirations for personal and professional development; and what can be done to build on experience and to develop expertise. This information forms the backcloth to the initial meeting, during which an agenda for a more specific self-appraisal is agreed, based on classroom observation and the collection of additional information.

In the spring of 1994, Kent commissioned the Cambridge Institute of Education to undertake a review of its appraisal process. Some of the comments made by teachers are worth noting:

> ...I was initially very negative towards appraisal, but now I think it is very good. I wish that I had the experience before, it helps you to

achieve individual focus: what you want to do; where you want to go. There is an opportunity to talk about yourself, which is very rare in teaching.

...it demonstrates that the classroom is not a closed area, but something we need to talk about.

...the opportunity to observe is a rare event. As a teacher I have not had the opportunity to see others teach. It is the best form of learning for me.

It is with this last observation that the rest of this chapter deals. Further information on the management of appraisal within local authorities and within the line management structure of the school, and the subsequent processes of staff development and formal review, can be obtained from the references cited at the end of this chapter.

Classroom observation within the appraisal process

The Kent appraisal process invites the teacher to agree on three areas of focus:

- the school development plan;
- classroom practice;
- personal and professional development.

The teacher may consider a variety of methods when collecting data but is required by regulation to undertake classroom observation. The Regulations state that there should be at least two sessions of classroom observation, each of which should last for at least one hour.

The Education (School Teacher Appraisal) Regulations (DES 1991b) state that the 'aim of appraisal is to improve the quality of education of pupils' (4[2], p.2) and the National Evaluation Report, *An Evaluation of the National Scheme of School Teacher Appraisal* (Barber *et al.* 1995), highlights the importance of observation in achieving this improvement: '...apart from enhancing the appraisal process, a regular and systematic approach to classroom observation in a school generates debate about teaching and learning between colleagues and across the school as a whole.' (p.62)

Figure 7.2 demonstrates the approach to observation taken by the Kent County Appraisal Team. The two sets of observations are divided into a *general* and a *specific* focus. The period of general observation allows the observer and the teacher to discuss a range of teacher activities and pupil responses, and consequently allows the appraisee and appraiser to arrive at a specific focus which will enhance the teacher's performance. In preparing for the classroom observation, the appraiser is asked to consider how best to create the right climate for the observation, to revise and clarify what is meant by 'general focus' and 'specific focus', and to negotiate and agree on the areas to be observed.

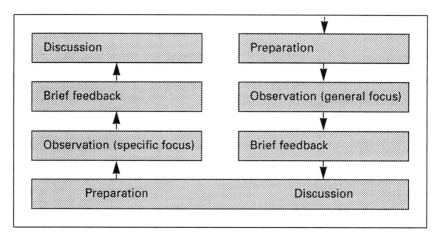

Figure 7.2

During the process of observation, appraisers are asked to ensure that observations are only used to record raw data, and to facilitate subsequent discussion. The appraiser is required to provide the teacher with a photocopy of the raw data, and asked to give a few words of feedback before leaving the classroom. Within the Kent scheme, appraisers discuss the raw data with the teacher within 48 hours, and the discussion focuses on:

- factual descriptions rather than opinions;
- the present rather than the past;
- *sharing* rather than *giving* ideas;
- alternatives rather than prescriptive statements;
- the individual's needs and how they can be modified.

The discussion concludes with a draft summary which can then be used to progress the appraisal into its next phase: target setting and the writing of the appraisal statement. Target setting and the strategies discussed for development are considered to be important outcomes.

The nature of observation in appraisal

From the description of the expectations placed on the appraiser, the process of observation in appraisal can be seen as essentially different from that used in either OFSTED inspections, monitoring activities, or forms of observation used in support of school self-reviews. The fundamental difference lies in the avoidance of judgements until joint discussions have taken place.

During their training, appraisers are asked to consider possible approaches to classroom observation, and to analyse demonstration videos which show badly managed observation. In these examples, the observer is late; disturbs the class on entry; interferes with the lesson by talking to the pupils about unrelated matters; is ill-prepared; wastes time looking for writing materials; and does not treat either pupils or colleagues with respect. Although the examples include exaggerated behaviour, the subsequent discussion indicates how close they can be to current practice. In one example, a teacher in the scheme had been given written feedback, in the form of a hastily written note tucked into the register, *before* the verbal feedback. The video training therefore encourages the appraiser to:

- be punctual, polite, professional and prepared;
- avoid preconceptions;
- explain to the pupils why she is in the classroom;
- agree, beforehand, on the mode of observation and the degree of the appraiser's involvement in the lesson.

The training also emphasises the need for the appraiser to give good non-verbal support to the teacher by using appropriate body language.

Another important part of the training programme is the appraiser's comment on lessons observed on video prior to a discussion of the methodology promoted by the Kent Appraisal Team. Appraisers are asked to view the video material, make notes and then comment in group discussions. At this point, comment may be negative in referring to such areas as: relationships between teachers and pupils; pupil involvement; the interest level of pupils; evidence of planning; the degree of differentiation achieved; attitudes; off task behaviours; and general control and discipline.

The training materials and sessions in Kent have shown that, when using observation schedules based on similar headings, teachers will concentrate on the negative rather than record what actually happens. In order to overcome this difficulty, they are encouraged to record raw data only,

109

which they are asked to share immediately after the lesson in order to temper critical judgement. The process, therefore, is that the observer *records* what is happening, *agrees* what has happened, *reflects* (with the teacher) on what has been recorded, and finally *encourages* her to interpret the information. The process is known as 'deferred judgement', i.e. the judgement is moved to the teacher from the appraiser; a very different process from that used by OFSTED teams. The following, used in the training materials for Kent appraisers, demonstrates the desired *neutral* tone of the recording. In addition to actions, questions are recorded where possible, and pupils' names are used to denote whether or not a boy or a girl has answered or *to what degree* he or she has answered the questions. Once teachers have become accustomed to this method of recording they, in the confines of an appropriate appraiser/appraisee relationship, become confident in identifying their own needs for improvement.

The manner in which this lesson was conducted could give rise to negative judgements on the part of the observer. The manner of recording, however, which is essentially *time sampling*, avoids this problem. It helps to raise the consciousness of what is happening in the classroom in a non-threatening way and, since it is not possible to record everything, allows the observer to focus on previously agreed phases or aspects of the lesson.

Recording raw data in this way allows the teacher and the observer to discuss what actually took place and to prepare a statement which recognises the teacher's strengths as well as identifying areas for improvement. In the following example of an appraisal-observation statement derived from a different set of raw data, the agreed focus for the time sampling is on the teacher's questions and start up exercises. The presentation of the raw data allows the teacher a degree of self-evaluation and the statement reflects the subsequent discussion between appraiser and appraisee.

Observation Appraisal Statement

Area of focus
It was agreed that the two classroom observations should be so organised that one built upon the other. Consequently two lessons were observed, during which Bob introduced the class to fractions: first to 'halves', then to 'quarters'.

Main areas of feedback on the above
1) Considering the constraints placed upon Bob by teaching infants in a mobile classroom, he is to be congratulated on the use he has made of the available space. The division of the room into a desk work area and an area for more informal work was particularly effective.

Time (minutes)	Record of raw data
0.00	*Class seated in rows; teacher at the front; exercise books on desks; teacher's statement about the League of Nations; chalk in hand; puts title, 'League of Nations' on board; class copies.* **Question:** 'Has anyone got a ruler?' **Corrected to:** 'Does anyone need a ruler?' *Various pupils look.* 'Mark, you'll have to borrow one!'
1.00	*Pens down; reflection by teacher on September work.* **Question:** 'What countries fought with Germany?' **Darren:** 'Austro-Hungary.' **Next boy:** 'Italy.' **Next boy:** 'Turkey.'
2.00	**Question:** 'Who fought with the Allies?' **Mark:** 'Russia.' **Henry:** 'France.' *Two groups in opposition.* *Teacher refers to cartoon.* **Question:** 'What is it?' **David:** 'Balance of power.'
3.00	**Teacher's** explanation of the balance of power; *class listen.* **Teacher's rhetorical question:** 'It didn't work did it? Resulted in WW1. Ended 1918. Devastation.' *Teacher suggested the need for a new order to keep the peace.*
4.00	**Teacher:** 'Look at me, Darren.' **Teacher:** 'Who was the American President?' **Mark:** 'Woodrow Wilson.' **Teacher:** 'I'll not ask you about the League of Nations because I know you don't know.'
5.00	**Teacher's** anecdote of playground bully. 'Bash your head in if you don't pay. What could all of you do if this happens?' **Mark:** 'Attack them.' **Teacher:** 'You all group against the bully. Like the League of Nations.' *Pupils listening.*
6.00	**Teacher:** 'League of Nations, just like the playground . . . same basic idea.' **Class instruction:** 'I would like you in your books to write a short sentence about the League of Nations.' **Teacher statement:** 'The League of Nations is a grouping of nations who agree to protect each other against bullies.' *Class begin to write; no questions asked.*

Figure 7.3 Classroom/task observation; record of raw data
Lesson: *The League of Nations*

2) During the discussions, it became clear that Bob did not fully realise how good the relationships between himself and his pupils were. Particularly impressive was the control he exercised over a difficult pupil (Glen) who was always positioned close to Bob and received a lot of individual attention. The atmosphere in the classroom was relaxed, but the members of the class were clearly on task.

3) Bob asked that one of the areas of specific focus during classroom observation should be his initial questions and his start-up exercises. We agreed that the initial questions were good, as he sought out children who were reluctant to respond and included them in this part of the lesson. From the record of raw data, Bob himself recognised that there were occasions when an answer was prompted to the point where children responded by giving a wrong answer.

Appraisal and OFSTED

Barber *et al.* (1995) report that all interviewees considered that classroom observation was a central element of appraisal, and that almost all believed that they had been able to demonstrate a 'fairly representative' range of skills or had improved their skills as a result of the appraisal-observation process. The evaluation concluded that the process had increased the teachers' confidence and had helped them to promote professional dialogues. The report, however, also pointed to the need for improvement. Concern was expressed about the need to choose the areas of focus for observation more carefully. Where teachers had *played safe* in choosing areas of focus, the classroom observation tended to play an affirmative role but did not provide adequate opportunities for professional improvement. Despite these difficulties, however, the report concludes that: '...lesson observation has clearly been a major success and has perhaps contributed more than any other aspect of teacher appraisal to the improvement of professional skills' (p.18).

This optimistic view, however, is not fully supported by the TTA/OFSTED (Teacher Training Agency/Office for Standards in Education) report of September 1996, which suggested that current strengths rest on the opportunity given to each teacher to discuss his or her teaching and how he or she sees career development over the next two years. Although the evidence obtained about teaching quality from classroom observation is invaluable, in describing the weaknesses of the system, the report points to a lack of rigour in the appraisal practice, i.e. a failure to apply the criteria for the assessment effectively, or to follow up weaknesses. It points to the poor evaluation of the impact of appraisal on teaching quality and standards and of the failure to secure the role of the line manager as the appraiser. Target setting for teachers, it points out, has often failed to focus sharply on improving teacher effectiveness in the classroom and targets are not sufficiently specific, measurable, achievable or relevant. The report expresses, given the more reliable and valid forms of evidence now available, the opinion that lesson observation is not wholly effective. This conclusion is based on the evidence from: OFSTED inspections; internal evaluation (including regular lesson observation and self-evaluation); value added work; and external test results and teacher assessment. The report argues that appraisal should:

> ...contribute directly to the improvement of teachers' competence and hence to pupils' learning and standards of achievement; be grounded in the regular monitoring and improvement of teachers' effectiveness in the classroom; and ensure that personal targets set by and for teachers contribute to the improvement in performance of pupils and the school as a whole.

(p.5)

Clearly, the authors of this report believe that the current arrangements for classroom observation within the two-year appraisal cycle are too loose and lack the necessary rigour found in other forms of more regular monitoring of classroom performance. When one looks at the methodology used for OFSTED inspections it is not difficult to see why both the TTA and OFSTED have reached this conclusion.

In pursuing the quality of teaching, the inspector will ask himself or herself many critical questions, such as:

Do teachers have a secure knowledge and understanding of the subjects they teach?

They will look at assessment methods and the degree to which teachers, using a range of knowledge, are able to provide demanding and appropriate work for all their pupils.

Do teachers' high expectations challenge pupils and deepen their knowledge and understanding?

Inspectors will judge the match of work to the ability of the pupils and the degree of differentiation evident. They will consider what opportunities exist for pupils to take responsibility for their own work or to use resources. They will ask themselves whether expectations are set at the correct level or whether pupils share and understand the high expectations of their teachers.

Do teachers plan effectively?

They will verify that clear objectives are shared with pupils and that intention and outcome are matched. The lesson will be placed in the context of wider learning and within the range of teaching strategies evaluated. Issues such as continuity and progression, classroom organisation and the effective use of support staff will be evaluated.

Do teachers employ methods and organisational strategies which match curricular objectives and the needs of all pupils?

In contrasting this approach with that taken in appraisal, the TTA and OFSTED have concluded that teacher observation in appraisal lacks rigour.

The Kent scheme reviewed

In reporting on their evaluation of teacher and head teacher appraisal in Kent, Hopkins and West (1994), of the University of Cambridge Institute of Education, came to the conclusion that: 'One of the more worrying aspects of the teacher accounts was less emphasis on specific changes in classroom practice than on the personal benefits' (p.13).

Although many teachers mentioned that they had become more self-critical and had focused more clearly on their teaching and on differentiation as a result of their appraisal, most of their comments were concerned with general benefits and tended to ignore specific classroom practices. This is a response that might have been anticipated in the first round of classroom observations as, at the time of the evaluation, most teachers would only have experienced two, one-hour sessions of classroom observation, and few would have taken part in OFSTED inspections. The present position is very different. Not only have many teachers experienced OFSTED inspections, but are also into their second or third round of appraisal observations. Anecdotal evidence suggests that teachers now more fully understand the process and are, therefore, more prepared to contribute to the critical analysis, based on their own recorded observations and those of their appraiser. There seems little doubt, however, that by itself, the two-year cycle is insufficient to address the practice needs often highlighted in OFSTED reports. Given that the OFSTED and appraisal cycles are likely to be perceived as being too infrequent for the continuous progress of teacher development in the classroom, it is necessary to consider other forms of development within the school. Two such areas are regular monitoring and self-review.

Regular monitoring

A possible relationship between monitoring, through classroom observation, and appraisal is illustrated in the following case study.

This special school caters for pupils between 3 and 16, with moderate learning difficulties. There are 14 teaching staff, the head teacher and 13 non-teaching staff, most of whom are classroom assistants. Staff are enthusiastic about appraisal and there are well articulated links between appraisal, school development planning, school review and staff development. All staff (teaching and non-teaching) are invited each year to take part in a 'Whole School Annual Review', and to comment on a wide range of issues, indicating whether they view them as strengths or weaknesses. These issues are wide-ranging and include: curriculum balance; methods of grouping pupils; internal communication; and budget allocation. Responses are collated and prioritised for specific review and, at a subsequent staff meeting, they are discussed in detail. In the 1996 review, for example, 20 items were identified including: aspects of communication between staff; the deployment of classroom assistants; and homework policy. They were then linked to the initiatives identified by the Senior Management Team and included in a revision of the School Development Plan. The Staff Development Policy ensures that this process is embedded into the two-year appraisal cycle. When negotiating his or her targets, the appraisee is fully aware of the priorities of the school and, similarly, individual targets are aggregated to inform the next stage of review.

The appraisal scheme was considered very successful but the head teacher was unhappy with the infrequent classroom observation within the cycle, as it did not, in his view, guarantee consistent practice in policies and schemes of work. Initially, there was resistance to the idea of more regular monitoring and its introduction took two years from initial discussions to its implementation. Gradually, staff were persuaded of its necessity through discussion and in-service activities. Finally, a staff development day was arranged using an SEN Consultant to work with the staff on an agreed schedule. An agreement was reached with all staff on a management process which required the head teacher to observe and give feedback to members of the Senior Management Team; in turn, they were required to observe members of their own line-management team. The school has now reached a point where staff are observed 'unannounced' each term, i.e. the teacher is not made aware of the 'observation' in advance. A pro forma, detailing the evidence in relation to the eight areas agreed by the staff, is completed for each observation. Items, such as planning, relationships with pupils, the suitability of the task, the variety of learning experiences, pupil achievement, assessment, resources and the suitability of accommodation for the activity, are included. This record sheet also includes prompts for observation. For example, among other indicators, it is expected that under 'Planning' there will be evidence of a teacher plan (linked to a scheme of work) and a daily log indicating preparation.

As a consequence, the school has changed its approach to classroom observation within appraisal. The two-year cycle remains, but the teacher has the option, at the appropriate time, of either a classroom observation as outlined in the appraisal scheme (i.e. using deferred judgement) or drawing on the data from the monitoring visit to stimulate discussion and to inform target setting. To date, staff are unanimously opting for the latter, and it is interesting to note that this school has recently undergone an OFSTED inspection and received an excellent report, particularly in the areas of 'Teaching' and 'Learning'.

Self-review

A number of LEAs, private consultancies, and national bodies (such as the National Foundation for Educational Research) now offer schools opportunities for self-review within which observation plays a significant part. In Kent, for example, the supported school self-review programme (already participated in by a large number of schools) offers lesson observation as one of a number of training programmes leading to aspects of self-review, which concentrate on the key elements of teaching and learning. The Kent *Supported School Self-review* (1996) training module 'Classroom practice: self-review inventory', which is skill-specific, poses questions under the broad headings of 'Planning', 'Lesson management', 'Process', 'Environment', 'Monitoring', and 'Outcomes'. For example, under 'Lesson management' the following questions are posed:

- Has the lesson an interesting start, a development phase, and is it likely to reach a satisfactory conclusion?
- Is sufficient time given to intentions?
- Can I accommodate the unexpected?
- Is the work differentiated by task, resources, outcomes or groupings in order to meet students' differing needs?
- What is the intended sequence and pace?
- Are students clear about these expectations?

A structured observation schedule is used by the observer in order to allow both raw data and judgements to be recorded. Examples of the key observation headings are: 'Intentions', 'Interactions and emerging experiences', 'Benefits', 'Factors aiding or hindering intentions', 'What is realised' and 'New or revised goals'. The schedule also carries a section for post-observation feedback, discussion and summary.

Target setting

A structure for observation and the honing of the procedures does not, however, of itself guarantee whole-school development as well as class teacher development. The whole, in a sense, is greater than the sum of its parts. Horne and Pierce (1996) studied 200 schools across four local education authorities, over four years, and concluded that teacher appraisal often 'lacks rigour' and fails to contribute to the improvement of teacher effectiveness in the classroom. The central point of their argument is that appraisal should start from a system that enables appraisal targets to be based on school improvement priorities, and that such targets need to have clear aims and objectives within a coherent framework; current practice is 'too cosy and comfortable'. Further, where appraisal is perceived as separate, it is seen as a 'bolt on' burden which does little to improve teaching or learning.

The Cambridge evaluation of the Kent scheme also makes clear that there is more variation in the responses of teachers to questions about targets and developments in the school, than in any other area of enquiry. The evaluation, however, was optimistic on the potential for target setting, as a means of improving, and having an impact on, school development. In general the more specific the target, the more impact it has on classroom practice. The evidence suggests that target setting, and its impact within the classroom, is more precise in second and subsequent rounds of appraisal. In the first year, targets are often led by the appraiser and, therefore, do not have the required degree of specificity in terms of classroom performance. Once teachers have been through one cycle, target setting improves because they realise that they are in control. In the context of whole-school approaches to the improvement of pupil achievement, however, it is not sufficient that targets should be specific, measurable, achievable or relevant at the personal level. It is important that there is a balance between personal development targets and targets which contribute to the school development plan.

Appraisal and whole-school development planning

In developing supported self-review procedures, some local authorities have endeavoured to link the positive features of classroom observation within the appraisal process with other aspects of school management. *Somerset Successful Schools* (1995), for example, encourages schools to develop a policy to improve the quality of their teaching as part of their overall management structure. The rationale of the package stresses that self-managing schools are self-developing schools and are thus self-evaluating schools. Each management policy strand (and there are seven under the heading of 'Curriculum') contains an overall rationale, aim, and a set of objectives, each of which is broken down into success indicators with evidence, judgements and targets. It is interesting to note that the two example policies which accompany this material, centre upon staff development and the quality of teaching. The two are closely related, as is indicated by the following set of aims for the staff development policy, to:

- encourage and develop the quality and motivation of all staff;
- facilitate and enhance the development of the professional skills and knowledge of all staff;
- harmonise whole-school, team and individual needs in line with the school development plan;
- improve the quality of education offered to the pupils;
- provide opportunities for all members of staff to reflect on, and refine, their practice.

These aims are integrated within the teaching policy in order to produce improved teaching and learning as part of the school development plan. Examples of aims from 'the quality of teaching policy' are to ensure that:

- teaching is characterised by a sense of purpose and clear organisation;
- teaching caters for the needs and abilities of all pupils;
- teaching sustains interest and motivation;
- lesson management fosters an effective, orderly approach to teaching and learning;
- the evaluation of pupils' progress is used to support, encourage, extend and challenge;
- learning is enhanced through effective teaching in order that the pupils demonstrate that progress has been made in the acquisition of knowledge, skills and understanding.

The value of this approach lies in the success indicators set for each objective and in the guidance which accompanies the material. For example:

> ...planning and the pupil grouping system reflect efficient diagnosis of pupils' needs and contribute to effective learning... (p.45)

> ...pupils' responses indicate their reaction to tasks which they view as too easy or difficult... (p.45)

> ...teacher question and answer techniques demonstrate purposeful approaches to supporting, extending and stretching pupil responses and understanding... (p.45)

Classroom observation can be seen as stemming from teaching policy, which in turn is developed from the wider management structures of the school.

Conclusion

The national scheme of school teacher appraisal was originally conceived in a context substantially different from that of today. Significant developments (the most important of which were the introduction of the National Curriculum, a national assessment system, the publication of performance tables and a national approach to inspection) are well documented in the TTA/OFSTED Review. Through the introduction of Local Management of Schools (LMS), schools have become more autonomous, a development which has been reinforced by the delegation of monies for support and training through the Standards Fund. In addition, schools, and particularly head teachers, have become more informed about, and committed to, the findings of research on school effectiveness and school improvement. In this context, schools are now beginning to see themselves as 'learning organisations' or 'thinking schools' (Ainscow *et al.* 1994). The current appraisal system, and the approach to observation contained within it, is likely to be revised in the light of these changes, and of more recent moves to introduce legislation on target setting for schools. Many of the characteristics of effective schools described in the OFSTED publication *Governing Bodies and Effective Schools* (1996) can be found in the appraisal process. The key issue, therefore, is not so much whether the scheme should be continued but how it can be improved. The national evaluation report leaves us in no doubt as to the three crucial elements of a learning organisation to which appraisal can contribute:

- *classroom observation* and, to quote the report,

  ...from a management perspective, it is difficult to see how managers can have confidence that policies are being effectively put into practice without there being a culture which involves classroom observation and a sharing of classroom practice.

  (p.62)

- *the appraisal interview* provides individual teachers with a focus on school development planning, policy information and prioritisation which would not otherwise be possible.

- *target setting*, which the national evaluation describes as,

  ...the process by which the broad aspirations and needs of teachers on the one hand and the development goals of the school on the other are combined and turned into practical, achievable objectives.

  (p.62)

What is clear from the different approaches to classroom observation discussed in this chapter is that different ways of observing classrooms are required for different purposes. The use of raw data and the interpretation of classroom observation within the appraisal cycle are not the same as lesson observation in the context of an institutional OFSTED inspection. Neither are they the same as the monitoring of policies and practices, or the development of specific aspects of the school's responses to teaching and learning through supported school self-review. It is likely that all these forms of observation will be required at some time by the school. It will be important, therefore, to keep the various needs expressed by them in balance.

References

Ainscow, M., Hopkins, D., Southworth, G. and West, M. (1994) *Creating the Conditions for School Improvement*. London: David Fulton Publishers.

Barber, M., Evans, A. and Johnson, M. (1995) *An Evaluation of the National Scheme of School Teacher Appraisal*. London: DfE.

Department of Education and Employment (1995) *Governing Bodies and Effective Schools*. London: DfEE.

Department of Education and Employment (1997) *Excellence in Schools*. London: DfEE.

Department of Education and Science (1983) *Teaching Quality*. London: DES.

Department of Education and Science (1985) *Better Schools*. London: DES.

Department of Education and Science (1989) *School Teacher Appraisal: a National Framework*. London: DES.

Department of Education and Science (1991a) *School Teacher Appraisal* (Circular 12/91). London: DES.

Department of Education and Science (1991b) *The Education (School Teacher Appraisal) Regulations* (Statutory Instruments). London: DES.

Her Majesty's Inspectorate (1985) *Quality in Schools: Evaluation and Appraisal* (Occasional Paper). London: DES.

Hopkins, D. and West, M. (1994) *Kent County Council: Evaluation of Teacher and Headteacher Appraisal*. Cambridge: University of Cambridge Institute of Education.

Horne, H. and Pierce, A. (1996) *A Practical Guide to Staff Development and Appraisal*. London: Kogan Page.

House of Commons (1990) *Hansard* (December). London.

Kent County Council Education Support Services (1996) *Code of Conduct for OFSTED Inspections*. Maidstone: Kent County Council.

Kent Education Department (1996) *Supported School Self-Review* (Classroom Observation Training Module). Maidstone: Kent County Council.

Kent Education Department (1996) *The Kent Appraisal Scheme for Teachers and Headteachers* (Appraisal Documentation). Maidstone: Kent County Council.

National Foundation for Educational Research (1995) *Classroom Observation: Briefing and Sample Schedules*. Slough: NFER.

Somerset Education Development Service (1995) *Somerset Successful Schools*. Taunton: Somerset County Council.

Teacher Training Agency and Office for Standards in Education (1996) *Review of Headteacher and Teacher Appraisal* (Summary of Evidence). London: TTA/OFSTED.

Chapter 8

Conclusion

Christina Tilstone

The use of observation in schools poses ethical issues, a consideration of which may lead to changes to practice and, therefore, it is appropriate that this final chapter should deal with the practical implications.

The identification of ethical issues in research, particularly in action research, the importance given to the formulation of principles, and the adoption of agreed procedures have been well documented in the literature (see, for example, Burgess 1989). Ethical issues are implicit in the problems investigated and the methods used to obtain data, and consequently researchers such as Frankfort-Nachmias and Nachmias (1996) give detailed information on how they may arise. They suggest that ethical issues stem from:

- the research problem itself (i.e. genetic engineering, determinants of intelligence, programme evaluation);
- the settings in which the research takes place (hospitals, schools, government agencies);
- the procedures needed to implement the research design;
- the methods of data collection;
- the participants or 'subjects' (people with Aids, schoolchildren, politicians);
- the reason for the data collection (personal information, recruitment practices).

Although *observation* is a main sources of data collection, the ethical issues surrounding its use are only fleetingly referred to in the literature; a strange situation when it could be interpreted as a means of keeping subjects *under surveillance*. The following list highlights some of the ethical concerns and procedures most commonly mentioned in the research literature. Many of the items listed only apply to outside researchers carrying out their own identified research activities in school settings. This often requires the consent and involvement of practising teachers, but the central emphasis is on the researcher's own hypothesis, which does not necessarily involve practitioners initiating systematic studies of their own work. The list, however, provides a starting point for discussion and ethical considerations which have a direct bearing on the use of observation will be examined in detail throughout this chapter. The prerequisites of research practice, which take into account the ethical issues are:

- the informed consent of the observed or, in the case of children, of their parents;
- permission from the relevant committees or LEAs;
- the articulation of a participant's right to withdraw from the research;
- a recognition of the power relationship between the investigator and the investigated;
- confidentiality and anonymity;
- the wellbeing of the participants and a guarantee that they will not be physically, psychologically or emotionally harmed;
- access to relevant files and documents;
- negotiations which take into account the beliefs and views of the observed;
- a guarantee that open reports of progress will be made;
- an awareness of the effects of differences in religion and culture and social structure on the research.

As previously mentioned, specific information on the ethical considerations of observation is not readily available. A general statement is to be found in the British Psychological Society's *Ethical Principles for Conducting Research with Human Participants* (cited in Robson 1993) which takes into account some of the issues listed above:

> Studies based upon observation must respect the privacy and psychological wellbeing of the individuals studied. Unless those observed give their consent to being observed, observational research is only acceptable in situations where those observed would expect to be observed by strangers. Additionally, particular account should be taken of local cultural values and of the possibility of intruding upon the privacy of individuals who, even while in a normally public space, may believe they are unobserved.

(p.474)

As children in school would not expect to be observed by strangers, does such a statement pose an immediate dilemma for the observer? Are

123

legally under-age children, particularly those with learning difficulties, in a position to understand what is involved and therefore is it necessary to obtain their consent? The answers to such questions must surely be influenced by deeper considerations of the meaning of education, coupled with each teacher's responsibility to investigate the best conditions for the promotion of learning, the most desirable teaching strategies for the effective delivery of the curriculum, and the development of the curriculum itself. Such investigations require children to carry out observable activities in educational settings and centre on a consideration of whether the preparation for teaching and the teaching itself is *right* (see Chapter 2). The conceptual framework for the investigation, which arises from those deeper considerations, allows the educational experiences provided by the teacher to be observed through the behaviours of the children themselves. Such a position stems more from the ways in which the observers conduct themselves than from the observed themselves. Woods (1986), reminds us that the observer must: '... behave with tact, discretion and decorum, and flawless recognition of proprieties at all times' (p.56).

The words have a faintly Edwardian ring and it is difficult to imagine what Woods really means by 'decorum and flawless recognition of proprieties'. His passion for all professionals to act in such ways does, however, raise moral as well as ethical issues.

Within the research literature, the words 'ethics' and 'morals' are sometimes used interchangeably. Robson (1993) draws a useful distinction between the two by emphasising that although both terms are concerned with 'right or wrong' and 'good and bad', ethics are the general principles which govern actions while morals, on the other hand, involve applying ethical principles to the specific actions themselves. He makes the point that enquiry into practice was traditionally considered to be 'value free' or 'value neutral' and the task of the researcher was simply to describe what was happening. Such a perspective does not, as previously discussed in this book, recognise that the views of the researcher are inevitably entangled in the enquiry itself. The choice of the focus of the observation and the nature of the techniques used are influenced by the views and past experiences of the observer. Bias and prejudice are lessened by the systematic use of observation, but the process is intended to lead to 'informed judgements and to necessary changes to accepted practice' (part of the definition of observation used throughout this book). Making predictions which involve change can be interpreted as exercising an element of control over people, particularly when those people, by the very nature of their needs, are regarded as less powerful in the first place.

Elliott (1985) is among the many action researchers who view the act of teaching (whether or not it involves a systematic enquiry into practice) as an ethical task in its own right. He considers teaching as an action which 'enables understanding' and argues that:

> ...teachers have a responsibility for the quality of provision they make for learning, for establishing conditions which *enable* rather than *produce* understanding. Whether pupils learn what they are *enabled to learn* by their teachers is their responsibility. In contrast, the idea of *producing understanding* suggests a passive process over which learners exercise little control.
>
> (p.250; Elliott's emphasis)

If one accepts Elliott's definition of teaching, learners are immediately placed in a position of some power. 'Enabling pupils to learn' not only suggests an element of control on the part of each learner, but specifies an educational action which *guides* rather than *dictates* each teacher's behaviour. As Burden (1997) points out, such a perspective places great emphasis on education as an active process. He takes up Elliott's point and stresses that such a process is a far cry from one in which knowledge is transmitted from 'powerful-all-knowing adults to passively recipient pupils' (p.144). When systematic observation becomes a factor in 'enabling pupils to learn' it is easier to consider the pupils under scrutiny as 'producers' of data, rather than the 'subjects' of data collection (Davies 1985). The concept of 'producers' of data suggests participation, and affords the possibility of the pupil playing a part in the decision-making process. As Scott (1996) argues, the nature of data collection itself is a social activity which demands a level of trust between the observer and the observed. The notion of trust is rarely articulated between the two, but is a basic ingredient of any partnership and signifies the beginnings of a democratic process. Such a position recognises the effect that the observed has on the course of action and, consequently, on the outcomes of their lives. Smith (1994), in wrestling with the philosophical and practical implications of empowering people with learning difficulties, urges teachers and others engaged with children with special educational needs to draw upon the self-regulatory process which forces us (the professionals) to:

> ...examine our environments, survey the possibilities open to us in particular situations, take decisions on how to act, and according to the consequence of our actions, revise and consolidate our strategies.
>
> (p.1)

If such revision and consolidation include viewing children as the producers of data, they immediately legitimatise one of the basic rights of the observer: his or her 'right' to be better informed in order to make educational judgements and to act upon them.

The rights of observers

Ethically, observation can be justified as a tool of enquiry within a conceptual framework which gives the practitioner the 'right to know'. Jenkins (1986) suggests that, consequently, the practitioner should, in the interests of children, become the 'knower who wants to tell'. He contrasts such a position with that of an investigative journalist who is basically a 'teller who wants to know' (p.202). However, by adopting the definition of observation used in this book, it is important to recognise that the observer is not just governed by the desire to *want* to tell, but rather the *need* to tell in order to ensure that the educational special needs of children are identified, their experiences extended, and their learning facilitated. Hammersley (1989) goes even further and emphasises that professionals have a 'right' to create knowledge and that to deny that right strips them of the knowledge generating abilities innate in all of us. Rheingold (1982) suggests that in recognising the 'right to know' observers should accept the *responsibility* to provide reliable data on human behaviour and the process of learning; a point made earlier in this chapter. Reliable data obtained through the use of observational techniques require systematic collection, reflection, decision making, and a re-evaluation of the conclusions reached. The experience should enable the teacher to develop a greater capacity for the discriminating formulation of ideas and judgements in complex, human situations, which in turn tests the built-in beliefs and assumptions she has acquired. For political reasons, Vulliamy and Webb (1992) stress that there are strong ethical obligations for teachers to share their findings with colleagues working in the same institutions.

The rights of the observed

An investigation into the educational experiences provided by the teacher does not necessarily require the consent of the pupils, but it is vital that they are not deceived, betrayed or exploited in any way. Observation may well be regarded as *spying* and, consequently, tact, honesty and sensitivity are essential if such basic rights as dignity, respect and privacy are not violated. The right to privacy must take into account the settings in which the observation takes place. As Frankfort-Nachmias and Nachmias (1996) remind us, the home is considered to be one of the most private settings in our culture, and intrusion into people's homes without their consent is forbidden by law. The extent to which particular settings are public or private is not always self-evident and the dilemma may lead to ethical concerns. As a direct result of the attacks in schools in Dunblane and Wolverhampton, such public buildings now have severely restricted access. It could be argued, therefore, that such a public setting is in fact private, and that to observe in such a context is an invasion of privacy. This position could result in the overturning of the arguments already made and ignores the fact that the teacher's task is to improve children's learning or, in Elliott's terms, 'enable understanding'. Webb and Vulliamy (1996) consider in detail the complex roles that teachers undertake in the light of the recent political and legislative changes. They highlight the key responsibilities facing professionals since the introduction of the National Curriculum and subsequent education acts and, as is to be expected, their snapshots of primary schools illustrate different cultures, staffing structures and ways of working, and give prominence to the stresses and strains created by the 'deluge of government directives' (p.164). Embedded in the evidence from their surveys is, however, the disclosure that the common motivating factor which binds teachers together in such diverse situations (and the possible resultant conditions of competition) is their enthusiasm for finding ways of monitoring the improvement of individual and collective classroom practice and learning, including the use of their eyes to collect evidence.

What does an invasion of privacy mean in work with children with special educational needs? Are there areas in the school where it is inappropriate to observe? An initial response may be 'yes' and toilets and cloakrooms provided as examples. Is it, however, unethical to observe and record the number of times a pupil with severe learning difficulties uses the toilet during a determined period of time in order to obtain a 'baseline' for a toileting programme which will ultimately help him to become more self-sufficient? The following observation, used to illustrate duration recording by Tilstone (1991a), took place in the cloakroom prior to a PE lesson:

> The focus of the investigation is the PE session. Sheila is concerned that not all the activities she had planned were achieved as it appeared that the children took an excessive length of time to undress

127

and put on their PE kit. Over a six-week period she systematically observed and recorded, using a stopwatch, the length of time taken to dress and undress. Her findings confirmed her suspicions. She then decided on the following course of action:

1) children will be given more opportunities in meaningful situations to dress and undress;

2) the more-able children will be paired with the less-able and encouraged to help with one aspect only of the dressing/undressing process. This will encourage the more-able to take on some responsibility for their less-able peers. The less-able, however, will not be denied the opportunity for some independence.

(p.121)

In this case, the observer's 'right to know' and the benefits that such knowledge afforded the children outweighed any suggestion of a breach of the children's rights to privacy.

Whole-school policy

By using observation in order to make informed judgements on their practices, teachers and other professionals undertake an inquiry. Inquiries in other professions follow strict principles of procedure and rules of practice and, if observation is to be taken as seriously as any other area of the curriculum, it should be supported by a policy document. Such a document should be owned by all members of the school staff and should reflect their agreed values, the ethos of the school, and the nature of the pupil's learning needs.

A suggested framework is:

- an agreed definition of observation;
- justification for its use (see Figure 1.2: 'The uses of observation');
- the ethical implications;
- a statement on how observation can be managed (for example the time made available for pre- and post-discussions during partnership observations);
- the resources available (video cameras, inside and outside partners);
- the in-service requirements;
- how the statement will be communicated to parents;
- a description of the ways in which the policy document will be monitored and evaluated, and by whom.

This list is by no means exhaustive, and the staff of each school will develop their own headings in order to promote the standing of observation in the specific setting. The value of in-school collaboration in the development of a coordinated response is a well documented strategy for school improvement (Fullan 1991; Ainscow 1995; Hopkins *et al.* 1994). Byers and Rose (1996) provide detailed information in four distinct stages on developing and applying policies:

- planning;
- formulation;
- implementation;
- review.

The planning stage establishes the purpose of the policy and identifies the professionals who will be most closely associated with its writing. This leads directly to the formulation of the policy itself and on to a consideration of ways in which it can be implemented. In the third stage it will be necessary to ensure that the policy document is put into practice and that suggestions are made for any relevant changes. The review stage should ensure that it is developed and extended as necessary, and Byers and Rose remind us that the aim of any policy document is to assist schools to become more effective and consequently 'they should be controlled by the school, and should not be the controlling influence of the school' (p.24).

As a starting point for the production of a policy document it is often useful for the staff team to agree on a set of principles which will influence both its writing and application. Fletcher and Gordon (1994) record a set of agreed principles by the staff of one special school which governed all its work. In addition to the basic human rights, which included respecting pupils' individuality and their privacy, two others principles are worth noting:

- to facilitate the development of personal autonomy;
- to strive for pupil representation.

Both imply the right to be consulted. *The Children Act* (1989), the *Code of Practice* (DfE 1994) and the UN Convention on the Rights of the Child, have emphasised the need for children to be involved in the decision-making process. People with learning difficulties have become increasingly critical of the ways in which professionals (including teachers) underestimate their abilities and undervalue their views (Tilstone 1991b; Miller and Davis 1992). It is, however, vitally important for teachers not only to listen to, but to respect, their pupils' views and to accept their opinions on the education that they are receiving in order to expand and develop a meaningful curriculum. Davie and Galloway (1996) trace the development of both listening to children and regarding them as true partners in all aspects of the educational process. Bennathan, in the same volume, cuttingly states:

> Surely the child as a passive recipient of services has had its day. Children have to be understood as interactive, as having a self-concept, an identity, which shapes their view of what is offered to them, in school and elsewhere, and which therefore must be taken into account as routinely by their teachers as it is by other professional groups.

(p.92)

Collaboration in observation is central to this process. Biott and Easen (1994) write about 'learning partnerships' and describe them as:

- a working relationship that is characterised by a shared sense of purpose, mutual respect and a willingness to cooperate;
- a framework within which each party's experience is seen as complementary and equally important.

(p.161).

Such collaboration leads to genuine participation in the learning process between the observed and the observer and, it is hoped, becomes a way of life. Observation, like listening to children, enables us to learn more about our successes and failures and helps us, as Charlton (1996) comments, to consider changes in our provision and practices.

A serious consideration of observation allows us to learn much from, and about, children and Cohen *et al.* (1997) remind us that the very nature of each child's ongoing development within the education process implies constant change and that the involved professional needs to be open-minded at all times. The skills of systematic observation lead to informed judgements about how a child responds to teaching and learning over a period of time. The education process means that each developing child's *tomorrow* is a little different from that child's *today* and in the words of Louis Pasteur (1854) '... where observation is concerned, chance favours the prepared mind'.

References

Ainscow, M. (1995) 'Special needs through school improvement: school improvement through special needs', in Clark, C., Dyson, A. and Millward, A. (eds) *Towards Inclusive Schools*. London: David Fulton Publishers.

Bennathan, M. (1996) 'Listening to children in school: an empirical study', in Davie, R. and Galloway, D. (eds) *Listening to Children in Education*. London: David Fulton Publishers.

Biott, C. and Easen, P. (1994) *Collaborative Learning in Staffrooms and Classrooms*. London: David Fulton Publishers.

Burden, R. (1997) 'Translating values into rights; respecting the voice of the child', in Lindsay, G. and Thompson, D. (eds) *Values into Practice in Special Education*. London: David Fulton Publishers.

Burgess, R. G. (ed.) (1989) *The Ethics of Educational Research*. London: Falmer Press.

Byers, R. and Rose, R. (1996) *Planning the Curriculum for Pupils with Special Educational Needs: a Practical Guide*. London: David Fulton Publishers.

Charlton, T. (1996) 'Listening to pupils in classrooms and schools', in Davie, R. and Galloway, D. (eds) *Listening to Children in Education*. London: David Fulton Publishers.

Cohen, D. H., Stern, V. and Balaban, N. (1997) *Observing and Recording the Behaviour of Young Children* 4th edn. New York: Teachers College Press.

Davie, R. and Galloway, D. (eds) (1996) *Listening to Children in Education*. London: David Fulton Publishers.

Davis, L. (1985) 'Focusing on gender in educational research', in Burgess, R. G. (ed.) *Field Methods in the Study of Education*. London: Falmer Press.

Department of Health (1992) *Guidance and Regulations and the Children Act 1989, Volume 6: Children with Disabilities*. London: HMSO.

Elliott, J. (1985) 'Facilitating Action Research in schools', in Burgess, R. G. (ed.) *Field Methods in the Study of Education*. London: Falmer Press.

Fletcher, W. and Gordon, J. (1994) 'Personal and social education in a school for pupils with severe learning difficulties', in Rose, R., Ferguson, A., Byers, R. and Banes, D. (eds.) *Implementing the Whole Curriculum for Pupils with Learning Difficulties*. London: David Fulton Publishers.

Frankfort-Nachmias, C. and Nachmias, D. (1996) *Research Methods in the Social Sciences*, 5th edn. London: Arnold.

Fullan, M. (1991) *The New Meaning of Educational Change*. London: Cassell.

Hammersley, M. (1989) 'On practitioner ethnology', in Hammersley, M. (ed.) *Controversies in Classroom Research*, 2d edn. Buckingham: Open University Press.

Hopkins, D., Ainscow, M. and West, M. (1994) *School Improvement in an Era of Change*. London: Cassell.

Jenkins, D. (1986) 'An adversary's account of SAFARI's ethics of case study', in Hammersley, M. (ed.) *Controversies in Classroom Research*. Buckingham: Open University Press.

Miller, S. and Davis, T. (1992) 'Beliefs about children: a comparative study of mothers, teachers, peers and self', *Child Development* **63** (5), 1251–65.

Pasteur, L. (1854) Address given to the Faculty of Science, University of Lille, 7 December 1854.

Rheingold, H. L. (1982) 'Ethics as an integral part of research in child development', in Vasta, R. (ed.) *Strategies and Techniques of Child Study.* New York: Academic Press.

Robson, C. (1993) *Real World Research.* Oxford: Blackwell.

Scott, D. (1996) 'Methods and data in educational research', in Scott, D. and Usher, R. (eds) *Understanding Educational Research.* London: Routledge.

Smith, B. (1994) 'Handing over control to people with learning difficulties', in Coupe O'Kane, J. and Smith, B. (eds) *Taking Control: Enabling People with Learning Difficulties.* London: David Fulton Publishers.

Tilstone, C. (1991a) 'Classroom evaluation', in Tilstone, C. (ed.) *Teaching Pupils with Severe Learning Difficulties.* London: David Fulton Publishers.

Tilstone, C. (1991b) 'Pupils' views', in Tilstone, C. (ed.) *Teaching Pupils with Severe Learning Difficulties.* London: David Fulton Publishers.

Vulliamy, G. and Webb, R. (1992) ' Analysing and validating data in teacher research', in Vulliamy, G. and Webb, R. (eds) *Teacher Research and Special Educational Needs.* London: David Fulton Publishers.

Webb, R. and Vulliamy, G. (1996) *Roles and Responsibilities in the Primary School: Changing Demand, Changing Practice.* Buckingham: Open University Press.

Woods, P. (1986) *Inside Schools: Ethnography in Educational Research.* London: Routledge and Kegan Paul.

Author Index

133

Subject Index